D199

D 28.56

The Encyclopedia of CARS

VOLUME SEVEN – Singer to Wolseley

The Encyclopedia of
CARS

VOLUME SEVEN – *Singer to Wolseley*

Chelsea House Publishers

Philadelphia

Edited by Chris Horton
Foreword by Karl Ludvigsen

Published in 1998 by
Chelsea House Publishers
1974 Sproul Road, Suite 400
P.O. Box 914
Broomall, PA 19008-0914

Printed in Italy

**Library of Congress Cataloging-in-Publication
Data**
Encyclopedia of Cars/edited by Chris Horton:
foreword by Karl Ludvigsen.
      p.   cm.
    Includes indexes.
    ISBN 0-7910-4865-9 (vol. 1)
    ISBN 0-7910-4866-7 (vol. 2)
    ISBN 0-7910-4867-5 (vol. 3)
    ISBN 0-7910-4868-3 (vol. 4)
    ISBN 0-7910-4869-1 (vol. 5)
    ISBN 0-7910-4870-5 (vol. 6)
    ISBN 0-7910-4871-3 (vol. 7)
    ISBN 0-7910-4864-0 (set)

1. Automobiles–Encyclopedias. I. Horton, Chris.
TL9. E5233 1997   97-17890
629.222 03–DC21   CIP

Page 2: Toyota RAV4 GX 5-door
Page 3: Volkswagen Golf Avantgarde
Right: TVR Cerbera

Contents

Singer

Great Britain 1905–1970

George Singer, born in 1847, learned his trade in the motor industry working at Coventry Machinists. He branched out to make cycles and tricycles and his first cars were the underfloor-engined 8 and 12hp 1905 models, built under licence from Lea-Francis and designed by Alex Craig.

In the following year Singer added more conventional two-, three- and four-cylinder cars. However, the company went into receivership in 1908.

George Singer died the following year and the company was re-formed as Singer and Co. (1909) Ltd. The date was dropped from the name three years later.

Singer relied mostly on White and Poppe engines, although it built some of its own, such as the 1913 14hp unit.

The miniature 1912 1.1-litre Ten continued in production for military purposes during World War I and sales continued after the war.

Right: 1931 8hp Junior Sportsman's coupé
Below: 1915 two-seater Singer Ten

Above: 1912 10hp Singer

The two-litre six was introduced in 1922 and at the same time Singer bought motorcycle firm Coventry Premier, briefly marketing the Ten under this name.

The Calcott factory was acquired in 1926 and, by then, production stood at 100 vehicles a week.

The Ten was now known as the Senior

Below: 1933 Singer Nine sports car

and this was joined by the 848cc Junior – the first inexpensive British car with an overhead-camshaft engine.

Singer became Britain's third largest manufacturer with outputs of 11,000 cars in 1927 and 8,000 cars in 1929.

Singer bought a factory in Birmingham from B.S.A. and commenced operations in 1927, making virtually all its own components, including bodies, radiators and castings.

By 1931, capital stood at £2 million and there were 8,000 employees. Many engine types were used until 1935, probably because managing director W. E. Bullock bought a number of designs from an Italian engineer.

Singer tried diversifying into commercial vehicles but production of tractors was eventually stopped because of minimal success.

The Junior was replaced by the Nine in 1932 and production reached 4,640 in 1933.

The designing of cars had become a somewhat complex matter, with stylist Charles Beauvais being hired from Standard, A. G. Booth from Clyno designing the chassis, H. M. Kesterton

being responsible for the transmissions and L. J. Shorter, formerly of Humber, working on the engines.

Singer's quality control was excellent – with final inspection by an ex-Daimler employee – and its cars became the most popular British vehicles in Spain.

Cars of the 1930s included a sports version of the Nine and an overhead-cam Eleven to replace the sidevalve Twelve.

Above: 1934 11hp Airstream saloon

Singer tackled the cyclecar boom with the Ten – a true car in miniature. The original Ten was launched with a three-cylinder 1358cc sidevalve engine, but by 1912 this had been replaced by a four-cylinder sidevalve of 1096cc. Production eventually rose to over 50 a week.

Sports-car sales were hit after the 1935 Tourist Trophy race when Singers suffered much-publicized steering failures.

A new version of the Ten was introduced to fill the gap between the Junior/Nine and the larger six-cylinder models but only 800 of these sidevalve cars were sold. A 1476cc sidevalve six-cylinder version suffered a similar fate.

Profits slumped after 1934 and two Coventry plants were closed in 1935. The £1 shares went down to 12s 6d in a reorganization which brought in ex-Hudson man H. M. Emery and led to a company name change in 1937 to Singer Motors Ltd.

Singer made about 5,000 cars in 1936, including the 9hp Bantam which was copied from the Morris Eight. The six-cylinder models were dropped and Singer lagged behind the 'big six' British manufacturers.

The war years saw Singer making components for military aircraft, shell cases and pumps.

Above: 1935 Singer Le Mans sports

Below: 1954 drophead coupé

The Nine model – launched just before World War II – went on sale again from 1946 and about 2,500 were produced until

The Singer Nine Le Mans was the main rival to M.G. in the cheap sports-car market of the mid-1930s. Its 972cc overhead-camshaft engine developed 45bhp at 5,500rpm and gave it a top speed of about 105km/h (65mph).

Above: 1954 SM1500 saloon
Below: 1600cc Gazelle convertible c.1961

Above: A contemporary Gazelle saloon
Below: Vogue saloon, new for 1962

1949. The pre-war Ten and Twelve were also revived and all production was based at Birmingham.

L. J. Shorter's SM1500 – with a cruciform braced chassis – made its debut in 1948 and production peaked at 6,358 in 1952.

Singer was bought by William Rootes' company in 1955 – Rootes, himself, served his apprenticeship with Singer – in a deal involving £235,000 cash plus shares.

The Rootes influence soon became apparent with the Singer Gazelle, based on the Hillman Minx, being introduced in 1957.

Badge-engineering became the norm with the Vogue, a Humber Sceptre derivative, and the Chamois, based on the Hillman Imp.

The Singer name was dropped in 1970 with Chrysler, Rootes' new owner, concentrating on other marques.

Above: 1965 Gazelle, enlarged to 1725cc   *Below: Singer Chamois Sport, c.1966*

Spyker

Holland
1900 to 1927

Jacobus Spijker and his younger brother Hendrik decided to call their cars 'Spyker's – spelt thus to aid foreign sales. Their factory at Trompenburg made cars from 1900 to 1927 and was Holland's only car manufacturer up to the outbreak of World War I.

A financial crisis in 1906 prompted Hendrik to visit their British agent and best customer to raise a loan. Spyker's entire 1904–06 output had been exported to Britain. On Hendrik's return journey to Holland with the agent a gale flung the steamer ashore. It broke up and both men perished.

To spread the Spyker name, Jacobus agreed to provide Charles Godard from Burgundy with a four-cylinder 15hp model adapted with low gears and high wheels to tackle one of motoring's greatest adventures of all time – the Peking-to-Paris race of 1907.

The open car performed extremely well and was a potential winner, but intrigue

Above: Brighton 1905. A four-wheel-drive Spyker (left) challenges a Thorneycroft.

Right: 1903 four-wheel-drive 50hp racer

Below: A 1905 version of the four-cylinder tourer which had a 2½-litre engine, three-speed gearbox and semi-elliptic leaf-spring suspension. Such a car starred in the film Genevieve made in 1953.

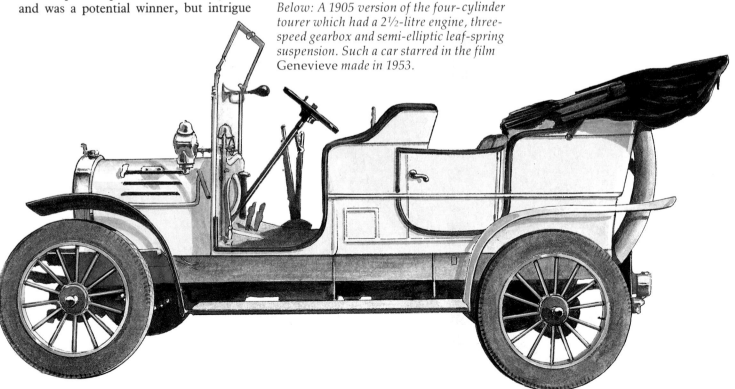

and Godard's cavalier method of raising money led to his arrest before the race was finished. Another driver got the car to Paris, but the resulting publicity did not help Jacobus. Three weeks after the race had ended, a shareholders' meeting removed him from the board.

On 1 April 1908 the company was declared bankrupt, but four months later, was reconstructed with new directors and went on to flourish, producing many fine cars including taxis, many plying the streets of London. From 1906 to 1916 Spyker made cars with no less than 20 different four-cylinder engine specifications.

During World War I Spyker branched out to produce aircraft and the company's post-war cars were influenced by this, the 5.7-litre Maybach-engined C4 designed by aircraft engineer Fritz Koolhoven having vestigial tail sections, for example. It was called the 'Aerocoque'.

Spyker also attempted to market Mathis 1.2-litre cars under its own name and to assemble American-made trucks. This expansion and fragmentation of resources proved to be the company's downfall and it went out of business in 1927.

Squire

Great Britain
1934–1936

Adrian Squire, like many young men since, dreamed of designing and building his own car while he was still at school, but by 1934 – when he was still only 24 – it was a tangible reality. Sadly, no more than 15 cars were ever built – 12 by Squire himself and three by Val Zethrin who bought the company when it was liquidated in July 1936 – but as a car designed and built to the highest possible standards, regardless of price, it remains one of the real milestones in British motoring history.

After leaving school, Squire enrolled as an electrical engineering student, but after only a year he joined Bentley as an apprentice. In September 1929 he joined M.G. at Abingdon, then two years later he and G.F.A. Manby-Colegrave established Remenham Hill Filling Station near Henley-on-Thames.

This was undoubtedly the first step towards the Squire sports car; the next was the announcement in 1932 of a brand-new engine from British Anzani. With a capacity of 1496cc, twin-overhead camshafts driven by a central chain, and a series of idler gears and twin Solex carburettors, it was just what Squire was looking for. The deal was clinched when Anzani told Squire he could have his own motif cast into the camshaft covers.

Squire's next move was to equip the engine with a supercharger – a relatively easy task since it had been designed with

1936 Markham bodied Squire 'Skimpy'

just such a step in mind – and then to develop the car's chassis. By the summer of 1934, a prototype was running with a 105bhp engine, E.N.V. preselector gearbox and hydraulic brakes, and the ensuing publicity resulted in a flood of enquiries, despite the fact that the Squire was one of the most expensive British sports cars of its day.

There were initially four models – open or coupé bodies on long or short chassis – all manufactured by specialist coach-builder Vanden Plas. Ranalah built some

bodies, too, and Markham of Reading provided the so-called 'Skimpy' bodywork which Adrian Squire offered in an unsuccessful attempt to gain sales when, despite that early interest, the car's high price put it beyond the reach of all but the wealthiest of enthusiasts.

The project was finally wound up in 1936.

The 1934 Squire used a supercharged 1496cc twin overhead-camshaft British Anzani engine. With 105bhp available, performance was excellent, and the car had a top speed of 160km/h (100mph).

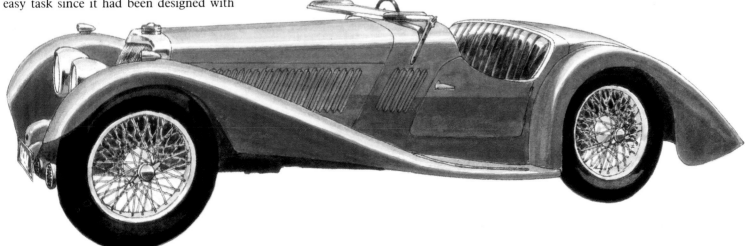

SsangYong

Korea
1954 to date

SsangYong Motors was founded in 1954 and initially specialized in commercial and 4x4 vehicles. It started its operations, like many companies, by assembling a licensed version of another company's vehicle, the Korando, a licence-built version of the Jeep CJ6.

In more recent years, SsangYong took an 80 per cent stake in Panther cars, the British specialist manufacturer. Later, in 1992, Mercedes-Benz started to show some interest in the company and took a 5 per cent stake, with an option to buy a further 5 per cent at a later date.

As a result of the Mercedes deal, SsangYong was contracted to produce 50,000 Mercedes-Benz 100 Trucks and an additional 80,000 diesel power units in 1995. These figures were expected to rise to 100,000 and 140,000 respectively by the year 2,000, with most of the diesel engines earmarked for SsangYong's own Musso

Above: SsangYong Musso 2.9D SE   *Below: 1997 SsangYong Korando*

Above: SsangYong Musso 2.3 Twin Cam   *Below: 1997 SsangYong Musso GX220*

luxury 4x4. A second joint venture that was planned between Mercedes and its Korean partner, was for the production of the V car, an E-class-size saloon to be built and badged by SsangYong.

The Musso was the first vehicle to be seriously marketed by SsangYong outside its native Korea. The unusual styling, carried out by a British design firm, helped, rather than hindered its sales in the West. The Mercedes diesel engine, which was initially the only engine choice for most western markets, also helped add credibility to the car. A powerful petrol-engined version arrived in 1996 giving very car-like on-road performance. Very competitive pricing compared to other large luxury 4x4s helped SsangYong's sales.

The SsangYong group is also the world's largest cement producer and comprises 24 companies. In 1986, when the car business really started, the company produced 5,759 vehicles; in 1994 they produced 46,375, representing an eightfold increase in eight years and by the turn of the century SsangYong plans further production hikes. The Musso's success gave credibility to the SsangYong name and paves the way for future models.

Standard

Great Britain
1903–1963

The first car from R. W. Maudslay's firm of Standard was a single-cylinder 6hp model built in 1903. A wide range of models followed, including large six-cylinder cars, from 1906, as well as smaller family cars such as the 9½hp Rhyl, introduced in 1912.

During the 1920s Standard built cars ranging from an overhead-valve 8hp model in 1922, to a 1.2-litre sidevalve Nine in 1928. Overhead-valve and sidevalve six-cylinder models were also produced.

Right: 1925 14hp Pall Mall
Below: The 9.5hp Rhyl of 1913

Above: 1926 Stratford all-weather tourer

Above: 1930 9hp Teignmouth

Captain John Black, formerly of Hillman, helped Standard to weather the financial storms of the late 1920s and early 1930s, and the company offered competitive models as it entered the 1930s. These included the four-cylinder Big Nine and six-cylinder 16hp and 20hp Standards.

During the mid-1930s Standard styling was very advanced, the streamlined saloons of 1936 earning the appropriate name of Flying Standards. Available with a range of engines (9, 10, 12, 14, 20 and later 8hp), the cars were fairly fast and extremely reliable. The pre-war Flying

Left: The first Standard light car was the 9.5hp Rhyl of 1912/13. This model, with a three-speed gearbox and worm final drive, was becoming increasingly popular by the time that war broke out in 1914. Electric lamps were available from 1915.

Above: 1934 Standard 12 (basic) saloon

when Standard's single new model – the beetle-shaped Vanguard – was introduced, with a two-litre overhead-valve four-cylinder engine.

In 1953 the notchback Phase II Vanguard appeared, as did the new Standard Eight, with an 803cc overhead-valve engine giving 26bhp, followed by the similarly styled Ten, with a 948cc engine developing 33bhp. This engine was later used in the Triumph Herald. A luxury version of the Ten – the Pennant – was introduced in 1957.

The four-cylinder Vanguards were updated throughout the 1950s, and a two-litre six-cylinder version was introduced in 1962. The same engine was later used to power the Triumph 2000.

Four-cylinder Ensigns were also built, with 1.7-litre engines from 1957 and, from May 1952, engines of 2.1-litres.

The Standard name and the company's own model range ceased to exist in 1963, although the Standard-Triumph concern continued under the Triumph name.

Below left: 1938 Standard Flying 8 Tourer

Below: Standard Vanguard Phase I, 1947 on

Eight was the first small British saloon to have independent front suspension. The Flying Twenty was available with a 2.7-litre V8 engine.

Standard components were also used in other models, notably engines in SS Jaguars and Morgans. The Triumph company was acquired by Standard in 1945, and post-war Standards and Triumph models were all to use Standard engines.

As with most other major manufacturers, in the immediate aftermath of World War II Standard marketed a reduced range of its pre-war models in revised form. These continued in production until 1948,

Stanley

U.S.A.
1897–1924

It is a well-worn cliché in the history of the automobile to say 'if only so-and-so had been a little more successful, everything would be different today'.

Probably the most use of that cliché has been on the subject of the Stanley Steamer. But here the cliché has been used wrongly, for the Stanley company was incredibly successful, at least financially, and while its steam-powered cars were sophisticated and well-made, they were quite simply not a match for the brand-new and exciting technology of the internal-combustion engine, which had caught the public's fancy rather better than the seemingly old-hat mechanics of steam.

The Stanley brothers, identical twins born in 1849 in Maine, U.S.A., started building steam cars almost by accident. They were initially violin makers, they dabbled in mathematics, and they invented various devices including an early X-ray machine and a photographic developing process – which Kodak bought for quite a large amount of money.

Above: 1899 Stanley Steam Car

The story of their involvement with automobiles runs like this: in 1896 they were at a fair when one of the new-fangled horseless carriages made an appearance. So unimpressed were they by its unreliability that they decided then and there to build a better one.

They ordered parts from various

Below: The 1911 10hp model was built under licence in Britain, at Gateshead. However, though sales were steady in the U.K., America's demand for steam cars had dwindled to almost nothing, and despite their fine engineering and many technical innovations this form of power was not to last.

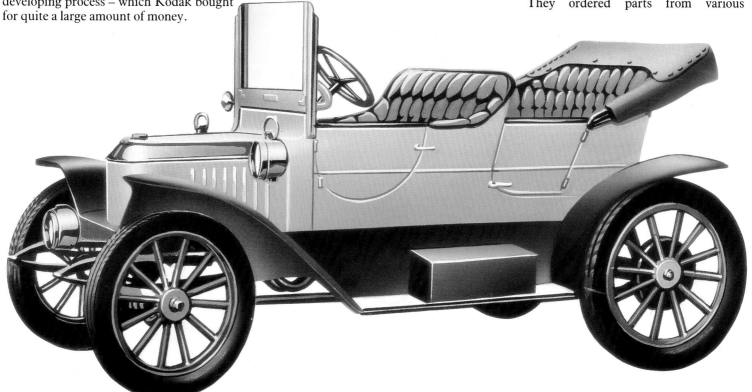

names two years later with a much superior car – thanks to the U.S. $250,000 from the deal.

Performance of their cars, with their firetube boilers and twin-cylinder engines attached directly to the back axle, was good; so good, in fact, that a speed record attempt in a streamlined car called Wogglebug went disastrously wrong. At 150mph (241km/h) the primitive stream-lining turned out to induce lift rather than downforce and the car took off, smashing itself to smithereens and seriously injuring driver Fred Marriott. Though Marriott recovered, the Stanleys never raced again.

The Gentleman's Speedy Roadster, a 1907 model, showed the benefits of this development, though; it could manage 75mph (120km/h). This was the downfall of one of the twins, Freelan, who died in 1918 in a crash. The other twin, Francis, had semi-retired by this time to run a hotel.

Above left: A 1904 steamer with tiller steering
Left: A 1912 20hp model
Below: The sophisticated Stanley 735 1920 model

After World War I the company was struggling, models such as the 735 convertible of 1920 attempting to disguise the fact that they were driven by steam rather than petrol, but orders started to come in, only to be snatched from the firm's hands by the recession. The company was run by a Chicago investment group until 1924, then bought by the Steam Vehicle Corporation of America which, despite the grand name, never actually built any steam vehicles. In 1927 it closed down, and though a brief revival attempt was made about ten years later it came to nothing. The steam car had lost its battle with internal combustion.

suppliers and in 1897 their first car ran successfully. But they were still convinced that they could do better than the heavy engine and boiler they had bought, so they designed and built a lightweight power plant, mounting it on runabouts of their own design which they used for personal transport without the slightest idea of selling them commercially.

After a Stanley beat several other cars in a race, however, they were flooded with orders and decided that maybe they should

go into business. They bought an old bicycle factory and proceeded to build 200 of the lightweight buggies. However, a publisher named John Brisben Walker convinced them to sell their firm for U.S. $250,000 on condition they didn't manufacture steam cars for a year. Walker and his partner Amzi Lorenzo Barber started making cars, disagreed, and ended up splitting the company into two different firms, leaving the way clear for the Stanleys to come back under their own

Steyr

Austria 1920–1940; 1953–1978

Steyr is remarkable in one particular way; its employment of some exceptionally talented designers resulted in cars that were exceptionally average. Though the company had some reasonable sales figures, it never achieved anything like the world-beating success of ex-Steyr man Ferdinand Porsche's Volkswagen Beetle (though it had a similar model) and never managed anything as revolutionary as ex-Steyr man Hans Ledwinka's air-cooled Tatras.

However, this is perhaps not so surprising when one considers that the company first started in car manufacture out of no choice of its own. It was, in fact, an extremely successful and long-lived armaments manufacturer up until 1918. It had been the biggest maker of arms in Europe, supplying the German forces with millions of rifles, machine-guns, military aircraft engines and various other mechanisms for institutionalized slaughter, until it had the misfortune to find itself on the losing side and facing a ban on armaments manufacture.

Below: 1924 Waffenauto Type II 12/40

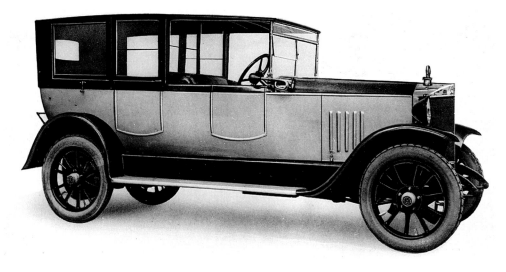

An earlier sideline in bicycle-making and the experience gained in aircraft-engine manufacture supplied the answer – cars. The first model was made in 1920, designed by the clever Hans Ledwinka, though it was a conventional enough car.

Ledwinka next proposed a small two-cylinder car for the masses, which was turned down, so he left to go to Tatra with the design which proved very successful. He continued to advise on the development of his original model, however, up until 1929 when another bright young designer, Ferdinand Porsche, joined the firm.

Porsche chose a bad moment to arrive. Only a few months later, as the Depression

Above: The 1925 Steyr VIII
Above right: Porsche-designed Type 30
Right: A 1929 Type 30 soft top

worsened and inflation spiralled, car sales at the expensive end of the market where Steyr were perched had stalled, and then the company's bank collapsed.

It was obliged to collaborate with the Austro-Daimler-Puch conglomerate, a move which forced Porsche to leave and set up his own design studio, though he, too, continued to design for the firm on a freelance basis.

In 1935 the companies merged wholly to form Steyr-Daimler-Puch, and while Austro-Daimler's production of expensive cars wound down, Steyr launched the Type 50, a cheap and successful Beetle-like machine.

However, war came round again and it was back to arms manufacture for the firm. Thanks to this, its factories were bombed to pulp by the R.A.F. and when the armistice was declared it returned to bicycles and then motor-scooters to survive. Later it built trucks and tractors and eventually, by 1949, was assembling Fiats and, a little later, producing cars that, though still Fiat-based, boasted the company's own engines. Hans Ledwinka's son, Erich, was by now in charge of the design department, and it was he who headed the development of the company's strongest seller through later years, the Haflinger four-wheel-drive mini-truck.

Steyr's last car, a Fiat 126 derivative, ceased production in 1978, although it still makes commercial vehicles.

Studebaker

U.S.A.
1904–1966

The last Studebaker rolled off the assembly line in March 1966, and ended a 115-year history of horse-drawn and motorized vehicle production.

The story began in 1852 with two Studebaker brothers establishing themselves as blacksmiths and wagon builders at South Bend, Indiana. After a slow start sales of wagons and carriages reached U.S. $2 million by the 1890s.

The company showed interest in gasoline engines as early as 1895, but initially only electric runabouts were produced, the first gasoline-engined car, a 16hp, appearing in 1904. Studebaker then sold E.M.F. cars for the Everett-Metzger-Flanders Company of Detroit, but after 1912 all cars were designed, built and sold as Studebakers.

In July 1915 Albert Russel Erskine attained Presidency of the company. Though remembered as being a ruthless and overbearing man, he did have the qualities to run a large corporation, and

firmly established Studebaker in the market, both at home and abroad. During the 1920s Studebaker was chasing the number-three U.S. sales spot; it had seven production plants (including a foundry and body shops); and it had an annual production capacity of 180,000 cars. In 1926 the company farsightedly opened its own 840-acre proving ground and three-mile banked test-track.

Above: The impressive 1923 Studebaker

Below: The popular Big Six 1923/4s

Below left: 1913 Model AA 27hp
Bottom left: 1913 touring model

In 1926 Delmar G. Roos ('Barney' Roos) joined the company and instigated straight-eight engines in 1928 and a less-complex independent front suspension system in 1935.

Below: The Erskine of 1926 was an attempt to make a high-volume small car for the masses; however, it could not compete with the Ford Model A. 'The Little Aristocrat' as it was dubbed eventually became just a plain Studebaker.

Above: 1929 – a classic gangstermobile
Right: 1935 Dictator Sedan

However, success was short-lived. During the early 1930s Erskine tried to operate as if the Depression had never happened and in March 1933 the company went into receivership owing U.S. $6 million in bank loans. Three months later Erskine, by now a sick and broken man, committed suicide. Luckily, under new management, with new financial backing, and the sale of Pierce-Arrow stock, Studebaker fought back, culminating with the success of the new Champion model. This sold 72,791 units in 1939.

During World War II Studebaker built military trucks, aero-engines and the Weasel – a tracked personnel-carrier powered by the Champion engine. After the war, Studebaker set trends, first in 1946 with its so-called 'coming or going' Starlight coupé, and again in 1953 with the sleek Starliner.

Again, prosperity was short-lived. The squeeze began in 1953 when Ford commenced a price-cutting war in a battle for sales supremacy. With higher unit costs and a small dealer network the

independent manufacturers simply could not compete. The last resort, it seemed, was merger. Initially Nash and Hudson combined to form American Motors, whilst Packard and Studebaker ultimately merged. Unfortunately for Packard, the ailing Studebaker Corporation rapidly consumed the former's remaining capital, and the great marque was effectively finished.

Under the direction of Harold E. Churchill, Studebaker pre-empted the 'Big Three' with the launch of the compact

Above: Commander Sedan of 1941
Below: 1948 Land Cruiser

Above: 1951 Hawk
Below: 1954 hard top coupé

Above: 1956 two-tone Golden Hawk
Below: 1963 Gran Turismo GT

Lark series in 1959 and actually made a U.S. $28.5 million profit. However, the Studebaker directors wanted to get out of car production, and in late 1960, amongst much bad feeling, Churchill was replaced by Sherwood H. Egbert who subsequently reduced the company's car-manufacturing proportion from around 75 per cent to 50 per cent. Fortunately, Egbert considered limited car production was viable, and developed the youthful and inspiring Avanti.

The break-even point for sales in 1963 was estimated at 120,000 units, but just 44,000 were sold. The model range was a good one, but prospective customers were nervous about buying a potentially orphaned car. Production reached 86 days ahead of sales at South Bend in November 1963, and was stopped for good in December. A desperate attempt was made to continue production of just cars and station wagons (with Chevrolet engines) at the Hamilton, Ontario, plant but, sadly, this ended in March 1966.

Above: 1964 Daytona Convertible
Below: 1964 Studebaker Lark

Above: 1963 Hawk coupé

The sleek Hawk GT of 1962 was a descendant of the mid-1950s Hawk range, widely touted when it appeared as one of the most beautiful cars of all time. It was styled by design guru Raymond Loewy.

Stutz

U.S.A.
1911–1935;
1970 to date

For two decades the Stutz Motor Car Company produced some of the finest sports cars ever seen in America. Harry C. Stutz was well known for his mechanical abilities and high standard of workmanship, and his first car, built largely from other manufacturers' components, finished eleventh at his local race-track – Indianapolis – in 1911.

Three years later, the archetypal Stutz, the Bearcat, was unveiled. It was an uncompromising racer with minimal bodywork and a massive 6.4-litre Wisconsin engine and over the next five years it won many races and broke several records, including the famous trans-American record, taking 11 days, 7½ hours from San Diego to New York.

In 1919 Harry Stutz left the company and started to build his own only moderately successful H.C.S. cars but in

Top: 1913 four-cylinder 60hp Bearcat
Above: Stutz racer at Indianapolis in 1913

Below: Introduced in 1914, the Bearcat was one of the most famous Stutz models ever built. Its four-cylinder 6.4-litre Wisconsin engine developed 60bhp at 1,500rpm and endowed it with a top speed of 137km/h (85mph). The last Bearcat, a 4.7-litre Speedway Six, was built in 1924.

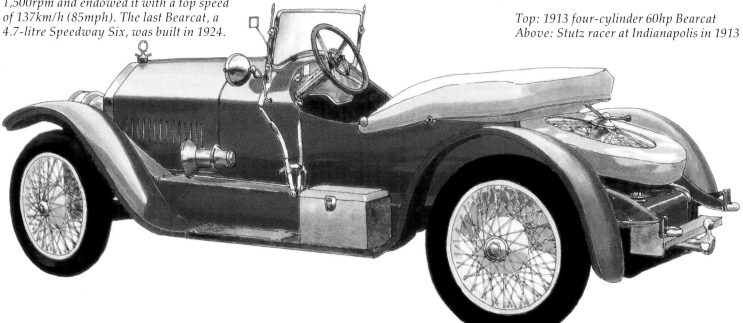

Above: 1919 Bearcat in road trim

Safety Stutz Vertical Eight with a single-overhead-camshaft straight-eight engine developing 92bhp at 3,200rpm. The safety features included a low-slung chassis, four-wheel hydraulic brakes and wired windscreen glass.

The Stutz Vertical Eight was one of the outstanding American cars of the day with the Black Hawk Speedster version

Below: 1927 Stutz speedster

Above: 1921 model year Bearcat roadster

1930 he died of appendicitis. Meanwhile, the company had been taken over by steel tycoon Charles Schwab and although Stutz started to build its own four- and six-cylinder engines, the basic car design changed little, with the last Bearcat, the 4.7-litre Speedway Six, rolling off the production line in 1924.

It soon became obvious that the company needed new blood and a new car, and in 1925 the Hungarian designer and great racing enthusiast Frederick E. Moskcovics, ably assisted by the Belgian designer Paul Bastien, unveiled the new

Above: Built in 1927 to make an attempt on the Land Speed Record, the Black Hawk Special had two 1½-litre supercharged Miller engines and an estimated power output of 385bhp at 7,000rpm. In 1928 it reached 327.5km/h (203.45mph) but crashed.

finishing second at Le Mans in 1928 and fifth in 1929, while in 1928 a similar car was driven at 106.5mph (171km/h) at

Right: 1928 40hp Sotheby Convertible
Below: 1930 straight-eight Black Hawk

Daytona, to set a new American stock car record.

By 1930 sales were beginning to dwindle, despite an improved version of the straight-eight and the introduction of a new, cheaper overhead-camshaft six, also marketed as a Black Hawk. At this time the American scene was beginning to be dominated by large V12 and V16 cars from Cadillac, Packard and Lincoln, so Stutz responded by producing its last great engine, the twin-overhead-camshaft eight-cylinder DV32, to power the new Stutz Bearcat of 1931. The new 5.3-litre engine had four valves per cylinder (hence the car's designation) with a power output of 155bhp, and not surprisingly each Bearcat was guaranteed a 100mph (160km/h) top speed.

Although the car's performance was terrific, the roadholding excellent and the build-quality superb, the price was simply too high to survive the financial rigours of the Depression and the marque finally succumbed in 1935, although light van production lingered on until 1938.

In 1970 the Stutz name was acquired by an American manufacturer who produced a somewhat ugly 1960s-style Bearcat designed by Virgil Exner and built in Italy by Carrozzeria of Modena. The cars currently available include the Bearcat and the Black Hawk, both with General Motors 5736cc V8 engines, and the huge Royale Limousine with its 6963cc V8 engine and optional hydraulically raised-above-the-roof throne seat.

Above: 1930 Stutz Derham roadster
Below: 1930-33 DV-32 Monte Carlo

Above: 1933 Type 29 Club sedan
Bottom: 1934 Bearcat G Type

Subaru

Japan
1958 to date

Fuji Heavy Industries, a vast and impressively successful concern, was formed in 1953 from the ashes of Nakajima Aircraft, a company which had been forcibly split up by the Allied forces thanks to its involvement in the war effort.

In 1956 Fuji launched Subaru with a moped, the Rabbit. Two years later the company produced the 360 minicar, which proved considerably less sensible; though sales were reasonable, it gained much notoriety in the U.S.A. for its safety standards and proved to be slightly less than ideal as an introduction. However, the firm ploughed on regardless, improving and developing the 360.

Above: Subaru 360 minicar
Below: 1966 FF-1 with boxer engine

In 1968 it introduced its first full-sized car, the front-wheel-drive FE. It was offered in various versions and sold well on Japan's home market, gradually taking off in the U.S.A. too.

Top: The redesigned 360, the 1970 R-2
Above: The Leone coupé of 1971

Below: Subaru's 1600 GLF 5-speed Saloon

In 1968 the firm was swallowed by the Nissan group and some of its plant capacity has since been taken up in building vehicles of that name.

However, in its own right Subaru has built several models worthy of note and attracting very respectable sales. The firm's four-wheel-drive vehicles, including pickups, are well respected and its Justy hatchback has claimed a corner of the small-car market as its own.

Above: 1600 four-wheel drive Estate
Left: The sporty 4WD Turbo Coupé

The company also has overseas plants, including one in New Zealand and one in Thailand, where its products are assembled for those markets; and its other interests include aircraft, commercial vehicles, trains and all sorts of industrial machinery.

Below: The XT coupé, which offers four-wheel drive and a turbocharger, is one of a number of Japanese performance coupés which offer very high levels of roadholding and performance in a well-priced package.

Despite posting losses like most companies during the recession, Subaru transformed its model range for the 1990s. At the bottom of the range was the Justy, which lost its three-cylinder motor and gained a new four-cylinder engine. It had been comprehensively restyled and was outwardly similar to the contemporary Suzuki Swift. Unlike any other Subaru, it was built in Hungary, alongside the Swift.

The Legacy, launched in 1989, replaced the aged 1980s model that had given Subaru its foothold abroad. It was campaigned successfully in Group A rallying in four-wheel-drive turbo form and sold well. It had smart and modern styling and a lusty boxer engine and in turbo form was very fast. To add appeal to the range, the Legacy Outback was born. With raised suspension and a torquey 2.5-litre boxer engine, it was a fun recreational vehicle and appealed to a new group of buyers, who were more usually attracted to the mainstream small Japanese 4x4s.

The Impreza was launched in 1992 and used a shortened Legacy floorpan. With less weight and the same power outputs (up to 280 horsepower) it became an extremely

Above: Subaru Impreza Turbo 2000 five-door

Right: 1997 Subaru Justy GX 1.3

Below: 1997 Subaru Legacy four-cam 2.5-litre, four-wheel-drive estate

Above: 1997 Impreza 2.0GL

Below: Subaru Justy four-wheel-drive five door. The Justy is built in Hungary

successful rally car, winning the championship on several occasions.

No one ever thought that the stunning SVX coupé would make production, but it soon hit the salesroom floor. Hardly a great seller, it was a great technical showcase for Subaru, and showed the world that the company was now making exciting cars, quite unlike the work-horse vehicles of the 1980s.

A brand new model came in 1997. The Forester, described by Subaru as an SUV (Sport Utility Van), was an exciting new recreational vehicle with chunky styling, raised ground clearance and a powerful 2.5-litre boxer engine giving around 170 horsepower. It looked like a cross-breed of a Jeep and a road-going estate car and entered production in the summer of 1997.

Top left: Subaru Legacy Outback

Top right: Subaru Impreza 2.0GL five-door

Left :Subaru Legacy four-cam 2.5-litre saloon

Below: The nearest you can get to the rally-winning Impreza is this Turbo 2000 saloon with a 2.0-litre turbocharged engine giving 211bhp

Sunbeam/ Sunbeam Talbot

Great Britain 1901–1976

Former sheet-metal worker and cycle enthusiast John Marston started the Sunbeamland Cycle Factory at Wolverhampton in 1887.

Eight years later he formed John Marston Ltd. to head his various business interests.

Charles Marston, a member of the family, started Villiers Engineering in 1898, making bicycle components.

John Marston allowed one of his former apprentices, Thomas Cureton, to tinker with a prototype car at the Villiers works.

The first offering – a Forman-engined 6hp twin – was displayed in 1901 and the first production cars were designed by Mabberly-Smith. They had De Dion engines, a strange diamond-pattern wheel layout and outward-facing seats and were called Sunbeam Mableys.

The motor department was taken over in 1902 by T. C. Pullinger, who acquired the rights to the 12hp Desgouttes-designed Berliets which were sold as Sunbeams from 1930.

They featured the oil-bath chaincases which had been perfected on Sunbeam cycles.

The motor section became the Sunbeam Motor Car Co. Ltd. in 1905 with a capital of £40,000 and within two years it was occupying two acres of factory space and producing the all-British 16/20, designed by Angus Shaw.

Pullinger left to join Humber and Louis

Above: 1904 12hp tourer

Below: 1912 12/16hp tourer

Below: Diamond-shaped 1902 Mabley

Coatalen became designer in 1909. He had considerable design experience on the continent plus a background with Humber and Hillman.

Coatalen joined the board in 1912 and was joint managing director with W. M. Iliff in 1914. Works manager Sidney Guy later left to form Guy Motors in 1914.

Competition successes led to improved sales and the £90 profits of 1909 rose to £95,000 in 1913.

Sunbeam built staff cars and ambulances during the war, as well as aircraft engines.

When the war ended, Sunbeam produced the 16 and 24 at the rate of 20 a week with most parts made on the premises. By now, the factory had expanded to 30 acres.

In 1920 Sunbeam was absorbed by

Above: In 1924 Malcolm Campbell took the World Land Speed Record at Pendine Sands, South Wales with a speed of 235.217 km/h (146.157 mph). The car was powered by an 18.3-litre, 350hp, V12 engine.

Left: 1924 4½-litre tourer
Right: 1925 Tiger Land Speed Record car
Below: 1934 Dawn saloon

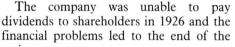

S.T.D. Motors Ltd. which included Talbot, Darracq, and commercial vehicle manufacturer W. and G. DuCros. James Todd was chairman of both Sunbeam and S.T.D. and Coatalen was the group's chief engineer and competitions director.

Sunbeam became deeply involved in racing and record-breaking but was best known for its quality and refined touring cars, some using overhead-cam Talbot engines.

The company was unable to pay dividends to shareholders in 1926 and the financial problems led to the end of the racing programme.

Experimental engineer/designer J. S. Irving and driver H. O. D. Segrave severed connections with the S. T. D. group.

Four-cylinder cars were discontinued in 1927 and the straight-eights and twin-overhead-cam six-cylinder sports models followed suit in 1930. So, too, did Sunbeam's attempt to maintain its position in the aero-engine field. Its last offering was a 1,000hp V12.

Sunbeam did better with a range of buses in 1929 which led to successful trolleybuses and the formation of Sunbeam Trolleybuses Ltd. in 1934. The firm was run jointly by Rootes and A.E.C. until

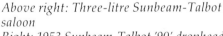

Above right: Three-litre Sunbeam-Talbot saloon
Right: 1953 Sunbeam-Talbot '90' drophead
Below: 1953 Alpine roadster

1944, eventually being bought out by engineering group Brockhouse and then being sold to Guy in 1949.

H. C. M. Stephens – formerly of Oldsmobile and Citroën – designed a new mass-appeal Sunbeam in 1932. Development cost £3.5 million and it was introduced in 1934 with independent front suspension and a 1.6-litre overhead-cam engine. But it failed to stop Sunbeam's decline.

The entire board of S.T.D. had resigned in 1931 following criticisms from shareholders over lack of co-ordination. A period of chaos followed which included a demand for the repayment of £500,000, secured to finance Coatalen's earlier Grand Prix ambitions.

Rootes had already revived Humber, Hillman and Commer. And it stepped in to salvage Sunbeam in 1935.

The Sunbeam name was coupled with Talbot – now also Rootes-owned – to offer a series of up-market and sporting versions of Hillmans and Humbers made at Talbot's London factory from 1938. They included the Minx-based Ten of which about 11,000 were made until 1948.

The Model 80 sold 3,500 from 1949–50 and the 90 about 19,000 until 1957.

The Sunbeam Rapier – based on the Hillman Minx – continued into the late 1960s, offering improved performance and

Below: Introduced in 1925, the three-litre Sunbeam Super Sports was one of the first production cars with twin overhead camshafts. Fed by twin carburettors, the six-cylinder engine developed 90bhp at 3,800 rpm, propelling the car at up to 136km/h (85mph).

Above: The new Alpine, launched in 1960

specification. It was later replaced with a fastback version.

For two-seater fans, Sunbeam produced the Alpine and a high-performance Ford V8-engined version – the Tiger. A Hillman Imp derivative, the Sunbeam Stiletto, was also offered.

The name Sunbeam was all but dead in 1968 and has occasionally been revived by subsequent owner Peugeot in a small way,

Above: 1964 Tiger rally car

such as with the Sunbeam Lotus, a Lotus-engined hatchback based on the Talbot Horizon.

Below: 1974 Rapier fastback saloon

Above left: 1964 Series IV Rapier saloon

Suzuki

Japan
1955 to date

Founded in 1909 as a textile company under the name of Suzuki Shokkuki Seisakusho, this company, which later became famous for its motorcycles, didn't enter the car market until 1955.

The first Suzuki car was the Suzulite 360 utility car, a diminutive and simply-constructed microcar. The front-wheel-drive Fronte 360 was the company's next offering, and was launched in 1967, to be followed a year later by the larger-engined Fronte 500. The Fronte remained in the range well into the eighties with only minor changes over the years.

The Cervo, also known as the SC1000 'Whizzkid', was the company's new car for 1977. This attractive 2+2 coupé used a three-cylinder two-stroke motor on the home market but was fitted with a more powerful 970-cc unit for European and other markets. By this time there was also a four-wheel-drive, Jeep-type vehicle in the range. Called the Jimny, this simple but rugged off-road utility vehicle was offered with various engines ranging from a three-cylinder 539cc

Above: For a long time, the Suzuki Jimny four-wheel-drive was the mainstay of the Suzuki range. It was also built in Spain

Left: The Suzuki Alto received a much needed restyle in 1990

Below: Suzuki's first sports car was the Cappuccino, first shown in 1991. It used a turbocharged 660cc engine

Above: Vitara 4x4

unit to a 1.3-litre four-cylinder, launched in 1982.

The four-wheel-drive market seemed a successful one for Suzuki, and in 1988 it launched the Vitara. This was a much more luxurious four-wheel-drive vehicle, designed with on-road performance in mind rather than mud-plugging. It became one of the most popular sports/leisure 4x4s, and gained a very fashionable image, especially when fitted with the full range of factory extras. The X-90 was a further extension of the on-multi-purpose 4x4 theme. Two seats and curvy styling placed it more as a stylish on-road cruiser than an off-road hauler.

Meanwhile, the road-car range had also expanded. The three-cylinder Alto had replaced the Fronte, and there was also the larger Cultus and Swift, both cars having sports variants. The Baleno, launched in 1995, was a competent and modern medium-sized saloon but was almost forgotten in the shadow of the company's now-famous 4x4 cars.

Above: Suzuki Baleno hatchback

Below: Rear view of the Alto

Below right: 1997 Suzuki Swift

Suzuki showed its first open sports car in 1989 at the Tokyo show with the production model arriving in 1991. Called the Cappuccino, it used a turbocharged 660-cc engine and a removable perspex hardtop. It was designed for the home market, but was very popular elsewhere, with many buyers importing the cars themselves.

Above: 1997 Suzuki X-90

Above: The fashionable Vitara was also available as a soft-top

Swift

Great Britain 1900–1931

Before beginning to build cars, at the turn of the century the Coventry firm of Swift were makers of sewing machines, bicycles and tricycles.

The company's first car was a single-cylinder two-speed voiturette. In early models, the de Dion-type MMC engine drove via a twin-pinion and double-geared crown-wheel system. Later cars, from 1903, had conventional transmissions.

From 1904 Swift produced its own twin-cylinder 10hp engine, also making three- and four-cylinder units and, during 1909, another single.

Above: 1908 25/30hp Limousine
Below: 1911 single-cylinder 7hp two-seater

In 1912 Swift introduced its 7hp cyclecar and a four-cylinder 10hp light car. The cyclecar had a 972cc twin-cylinder

Above: 1914 Swift cyclecar

engine and a three-speed shaft-driven transmission system. The engine fitted to the four-cylinder model had a capacity of 1100cc.

This 10hp model was built after World War I when Swift also produced a similar 12hp model with a two-litre engine driving the rear wheels through a four-speed gearbox.

From 1923, the 10hp and 12hp engines were updated by being fitted with detachable cylinder heads, making maintenance and overhaul far easier.

In 1926 a 14/40hp model was introduced with a new engine, and the capacity of the

Bottom: 1925 'Q' Type tourer

10hp power unit was increased to 1.2 litres.

Swift introduced a new 10hp saloon model in 1930, featuring wire wheels and a four-speed gearbox. The following year, the company produced an 8hp Cadet model. Unfortunately, however, the company was unable to compete in business terms with the likes of Austin, Morris and Ford, and it closed down in 1931.

During their relatively short history, Swift vehicles had earned a reputation for being strong, uncomplicated and thoroughly dependable.

Talbot

Great Britain
1903–1959
1979–1986

To sell French built Cléments on the English market a syndicate between Talbot and the Earl of Shrewsbury was set up in 1903. The natural conclusion was for the new concern to make cars under its own name and by the end of the decade two-, four- and six-cylinder Talbots were available.

The company's 20hp 3.8-litre car of 1906 is generally regarded as the first of the truly British Talbots. It was one of a growing range from the company's west London factory.

In 1913 a Talbot was the first car to cover 100 miles (160km) in one hour with Percy Lambert behind the wheel at Brooklands.

Right: 1930 Talbot 75 Saloon
Below: 1909 4156cc Talbot 4T

After World War I the Talbot lineage started to become somewhat complicated. In 1920 it became part of S.T.D. (Sunbeam Talbot Darracq) Motors. After that date Darracq cars made at Suresnes, Seine, France, were sold in France as Talbots and Talbot-Darracqs in England.

In 1916 talented Swiss engineer Georges Roesch joined the company and was responsible for the 10/23 model of 1923.

Two years later Roesch was made chief executive of Clément Talbot by Louis Coatalen who was in charge of S.T.D. Roesch produced the light six-cylinder 1.9-litre 14/45 overhead-valve model. A sophisticated and smooth design, it became Talbot's only listed model for 1929 and 1930.

Also known as the Type 65, it was followed by the 2.3-litre 75 and 90, the three-litre 95 and 105 and the 3.4-litre 110. Versions prepared for competition by Fox and Nicholls of Tolworth, Surrey, were highly successful, the assocation ending in 1932 when Fox and Nicholls decided to concentrate on Lagonda.

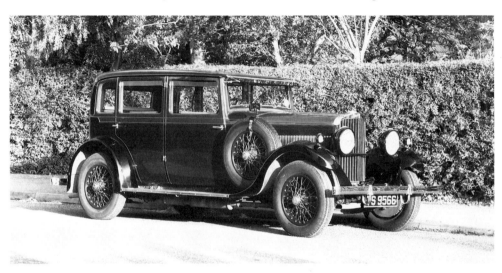

Below: 1923 10/23hp Talbot designed by Swiss engineer Georges Roesch. Based on Darracq, it was regarded as a fine four-cylinder car of side-valve design. Roesch followed up with an ohv six-cylinder car of high esteem.

Talbot finished third at Le Mans in 1930, 1931 and 1932. In the Alpine Rally Trials of 1931, 1932 and 1934 seven 105s were entered, all finishing without penalty. Alpine winners in 1932 and 1934 (jointly with Adler), Talbot also had class wins in the Irish Grand Prix, the Ulster TT and the Brooklands 500-mile (800km) race in 1930.

The S.T.D. group failed in 1935 and the Talbot and Sunbeam names were taken over by the Rootes brothers who added them to Hillman and Humber.

The inevitable cross-hatching of cars began, the Talbot Ten of 1936 being influenced by the Hillman Minx.

Roesch-designed cars were listed until 1938, but by this time Talbot's purity through its own design was now part of history and Roesch left.

Above: 1931 Talbot '105' Brooklands   *Below: 1936 Talbot 10 Saloon*

Above: 1933 Talbot 90 Vanden Plas
Right: 1938 Sunbeam-Talbot dhc
Below: 1936 3½-litre Sports Saloon

In 1938 Rootes renamed the marque Sunbeam-Talbot, fusing the two together. The post-World War II Sunbeam Talbot 80 and 90 saloon cars were well received by the British market, but the name Talbot was dropped in 1954.

Meanwhile the French Talbot factory had introduced a straight-eight 3.8-litre model in 1930. Few were made and the six-cylinder cars were the company's main source of income.

In 1935 Anthony Lago joined and used the six-cylinder engine enlarged to 4000cc to create the Talbot Lago Special.

Lago kept Talbot in France alive until 1959, producing a range of exotic machinery. His 'cross pushrod' six-cylinder engine won the 1937 Le Mans race and it was used in Grand Prix competition before and after World War II. His Talbot Record of 1946 with 4482cc displacement was to become a classic, winning at Le Mans in 1950. A smaller version, the 'Baby' Lago, was later

produced, and Maserati, B.M.W. and Simca engines were used to power Lago Talbots.

The Talbot name reappeared in 1979. Chrysler, who had taken over Rootes, were in trouble and thinking of backing out of

Above right: 1949 Talbot four-litre

Below: 1959 Talbot-Lago America Coupé powered by a 2476cc BMW V8 giving 125bhp. Claimed top speed 200km/h (125mph). It was first seen at the 1955 Paris Show powered by a 2491cc unit.

Above: 1951 Sunbeam-Talbot 90

Europe. Peugeot-Citroën stepped in and British Chryslers and French Simcas became known as Talbots.

A Talbot Sunbeam-Lotus hatchback won the 1980 R.A.C. Rally and the 1981 world rally championship.

Talbot in name had entered the 1980s but was destined not to last the decade. Sunbeam, Simca and Chrysler (still made in America) also added their names to the missing-in-Europe list, Talbot vanishing in 1986.

Below: 1978 Matra Rancho, Talbot in 1982   *Top: 1979 2.2 Talbot Sunbeam-Lotus*   *Above: 1981 2.2GL Talbot Tagora*

Tatra

Czechoslovakia 1923 to date

Though trucks and railway rolling stock have always been the backbone of this Czechoslovakian company's success, it is its cars that most will remember.

Of course, there is a good reason for this. They were extremely memorable, being both mechanically unusual and bodily very distinctive. And the genius engineer Hans Ledwinka put his idiosyncratic personal stamp on this firm's products, too – ensuring that they would be workable rather than weird. It is just a shame that so few Tatras have ever made their way beyond the Iron Curtain.

It all started in the mid-1800s in a small northern Moravian village called Nesseldorf, when a pair of carpenters and wheelwrights, Ignac Sustala and Adolf Raska, started a company producing carts and coaches. Business grew fast, aided by an expansion into railway-carriage construction, and in 1897 they moved into cars as well.

The motor car part of the firm was christened Nesseldorf and the first model, the President, was manufactured using a Benz engine. At the same time a truck design was started, and by the turn of the century a bus and an electric car were also being considered.

Though a racing car was built and successfully run using a Benz engine, the Nesseldorf company decided that it had to make use of its own engines. A year later it was able to offer three types, though these were at first not particularly good. Ledwinka took charge of the car direction in 1906 (rejoining after a sojourn elsewhere) and produced the S Type, a three-litre machine with many innovations for its day. Slightly later models boasted such features as four-wheel braking and overhead camshafts – before World War I.

After the war, which had found the company making mostly trucks, the firm found itself in the new state of Czechoslovakia. And not satisfied with changing its country of origin, it also changed its name to Tatra; a long-time

Above: A Type 12 of the Twenties

nickname after the mountains the development staff used to test cars in.

By 1923 Ledwinka had designed a small car for the ordinary man in the street, the Tatra 11. It was designed to be rugged and simple, and it succeeded brilliantly. It was victorious in competition and sales were excellent. By 1934, however, many variations on the theme had been tried and

Below: 1938 Tatra 57K Kubelwagen

it was time for another Ledwinka brainwave. The result was the Type 77, the world's first enclosed all-streamlined production car. Its variants, the 77A, 87 and 97, refined the theme while introducing different engines. But war was upon the horizon once again and before long the German occupation had forced the firm to discontinue car production.

After World War II the firm was taken over by the government and at first produced a trickle of pre-war models along with a flood of railway stock and commercial vehicles. In 1948, though, the Tatraplan was introduced. Basically a two-litre version of the streamlined Type 77, it was produced for only four years, mostly for party officials, before it was discontinued in favour of increasing lorry production capacity yet again.

The company bounced back in 1955 with the T603, a characteristically rounded design with a rear-mounted air-cooled V8 engine and improved suspension; a design, too, which was to survive until 1973 when the T613 came along, which had a larger version of the same engine and much more straightforward styling by Vignale.

No new models have been introduced since, however, and the truck side of the business appears to have gained the upper hand once and for all.

Above: 1940 Type 87, a futuristic oddity
Below: 613 Italian-styled body with V8

Toyota

Japan
1936 to date

Sakichi Toyoda ran a successful business making weaving looms and in 1929 sold the patent rights to a British company for £100,000.

His son Kiichiro used the money to set up a car department, having studied production methods in America and England, and the first car was launched in 1936.

It was an American-based model called the AA and used a Chevrolet chassis and transmission with a Japanese-built engine.

The Toyota Motor Company was formed in 1937, the name being changed to Toyota for several reasons including the fact that it was phonetically easier to pronounce and spell than Toyoda. The factory was located at Koromo.

By 1938 production reached about 2,000 cars, trucks and buses a month.

Truck output was 42,813 in 1941 and

Above: The first luxury car, the 1944 B
Below: 1955 RSD Crown Deluxe

soon afterwards a four-wheel-drive amphibian was added to the range.

By the end of the war the company had around 3,000 employees and production had been switched totally to trucks.

Car production resumed in 1947 at the lowly rate of 300 a year. The range included the Toyopet 27bhp light car and light four-wheel-drives.

Toyota formed Aisin Seiki and Nippondenso in 1949 to make electrical equipment for domestic and vehicle use.

The company had been seriously hit by losses and long strikes which led to the resignation of Kiichiro Toyoda.

The new management included Eiji Toyoda – who later became president – and Shoichi Saito. They had visited Ford in the United States to study the latest ideas and their enthusiasm paid dividends. Car production rose from 700 a month in 1955 to 50,000 a month ten years later.

Sales were helped by exports and, following the availability of the first English-language catalogues in 1956, Toyota enjoyed success in foreign markets.

In 1961, 3,932 cars and 7,743 commercials went abroad and ten years later the figures were 604,923 cars and 181,364 commercials.

A plant devoted solely to car production came on stream at Motomachi in 1959 by which time the one-litre Corona had made its debut.

The 1968 Corona was a good solid mass-market car with rear-wheel-drive and using a fairly aged design of engine – but it sold at a keen price.

The model proved a winner and sales of the Corona family reached five million in 1981.

Toyota's first mass-market car was the 1000 UP10 of 1961 which, in four-cylinder form, later became the Starlet.

The 1.1-litre Corolla, produced from 1966, became a top-seller in Japan.

Daihatsu came under Toyota's control in 1967 and the original loom company had, by then, diversified into making fork-lift trucks and hydraulic loading shovels.

Toyota exported its ten millionth car in 1971 and production reached 30 million by January 1980.

Traditionally, Toyota had produced rear-wheel-drive cars and the first mass-produced front-wheel-drive models were the 1.4-litre Tercel and Corsa of 1978.

Models such as the supermini Starlet and Corolla had already established Toyota as a manufacturer of dependable cars.

Above: 1975 2000, also known as Corona

Below: Crown Super saloon of 1975
Bottom: 1981 Land Cruiser diesel estate

Above: The 1985 Corolla GT was a much more sophisticated product than many of its predecessors, demonstrating the technological strides that the firm had made over the years. Engine development and chassis technology are nowadays knitted into the fabric of the company's products.

Above left: 1981 Starlet 1200 GL
Above centre: 1982 Hi-Ace minibus
Above: 1982 Tercel, an fwd first

Above left: 1983 Corolla 1.3 GL
Above: 1983 Corolla 1.3 GL with liftback

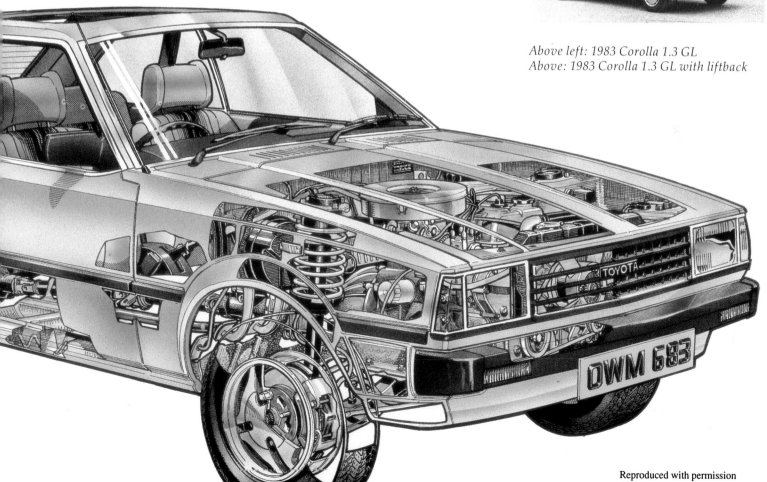

The MR2 of 1984 earned it respect in the world of technology. The mid-engined two-seater used a 16-valve 1600cc power unit which, combined with nimble handling, made it a tempting buy for sports-car enthusiasts, particularly because of its relatively low price.

A year later Toyota had reached another milestone when the Land-Cruiser became the world's best-selling all-wheel-drive vehicle. It was sold officially in 95 countries and unofficially virtually everywhere else.

Right: 1984 MR2, a sports car milestone
Below: 1984 sporty Celica 2.0 XT liftback

Below: The MR2 T-bar has superficial resemblances to its contemporary, the Fiat/Bertone X1/9. However, it is in many ways a more sophisticated car.

Top: 1985 four-wheel-drive Tercel estate
Above: Toyota's 1985 Space Cruiser
Right: 1985 16-valve twin cam Corolla GT
Below: 1985 Camry 2.0 GLi saloon

The sporting Supra of 1986 set new performance standards with its high-tech three-litre fuel-injected engine. Even more so when the Turbo version became available early in 1989.

Also in 1989, Toyota unveiled the third-generation of its Celica coupé, with controversially individual styling, and the second-generation MR2. Bigger and faster than its predecessor, the new MR2 is offered with normally-aspirated and turbocharged two-litre four-cylinder engines that produce 167bhp and 228bhp respectively.

Current production of all vehicles is in the order of one every four seconds, maintaining Toyota's position as the world's largest motor manufacturer.

Above right: The curvaceous 1990 Celica
Right: 1990 Carina GL five-door
Below: Today's sleek Celica GT-Four

The 1989 Celica is an example of what would in early days have been called a sports coupé or even a touring car: the two-litre, fuel-injected engine gave it a strong position in the sports GT class.

Above: 1990 Toyota Land Cruiser II

Below: Toyota's Supra is, indeed, superlative, boasting a straight-six, 24-valve, twin cam, three-litre engine. It marks a shift in emphasis from mass-market models towards the top end of the luxury and high-performance market.

Toyota remained at the top of the pile throughout the 1990s, and due to its enormous wealth was under no threat from the recession, unlike many smaller companies.

The sporting Supra was comprehensively updated for 1993, with new bolder styling and even more power. The 3.0-litre straight six engine now had 24 valves and gave 224 horsepower in naturally aspirated form and a

Left: 1996 Toyota Starlet

Below left: 1996 Toyota MR2 GT

massive 330 horsepower when equipped with two turbochargers plus an intercooler.

The Toyota Carina, traditionally one of the company's biggest sellers, continued to top the sales charts and was available in two forms: the Japanese-built Carina and the British-built Carina E for Europe.

Cashing in on the late-1990s trend for mini MPVs, Toyota launched the Ipsum, called the Picnic outside Japan. The compact body could carry six adults in relative comfort.

A larger MPV came in the form of the Sienna or Avalon. Based on the Camry, the Sienna was built at Toyota's US plant and used a 3.0-litre V6 engine giving 195 horsepower.

The Camry itself was also available in two forms: the Camry J, also known as the Vista, and the European Camry, with bigger, more powerful engines.

It was this tailoring of models for specific markets that helped to keep Toyota at the head of the worldwide market throughout the 1990s.

Below: Toyota Picnic mini-MPV

Above: Post-1997 face-lifted Corolla

Above: Short-wheelbased Landcruiser

Above: 1997 Toyota Landcruiser

Right: Toyota Camry Sport Saloon

Above: 1997 Toyota Celica Cabriolet

Above: Carina E, built in and designed for Europe

Above left: Toyota Previa was the company's first proper MPV

Above: The Hilux 4x4 double-cab pick-up was popular in Europe as a working vehicle

Left: Toyota RAV-4 five-door

Below: The Toyota Paseo 2+2 coupé was styled in California to appeal to American buyers

Above: Corolla four-door saloon

Above: The Rav-4 had permanent four-wheel drive but was designed for use on road. It had good performance and handling

Left: The Celica coupé had grown a little soft by the late 1990s

Tracta

France
1926–1934

Tracta began life as an exercise in the workability of a design and its creator made very little money from the venture. During the 1920s many French manufacturers experimented with front-wheel-drive vehicles, but none met with the same success that came to Jean Albert Grégoire when he formed the Société Anonyme des Automobiles Tracta in 1926. Finance for this project was provided by the wealthy Pierre Fenaille.

Work began at Grégoire's Garage des Chantiers at Versailles, shortly moving to Asnières, in the Seine district of Paris. His first design was a two-seater powered by an S.C.A.P. engine, which he displayed to the public for the first time at the 1927 Paris Salon. That year he also began racing. In fact, Grégoire's company was unusual in that his successful forays into competition came after the launch of his production sports cars, which were, therefore, not race-developed models. In total, 142 of this type of Tracta were produced.

Grégoire managed to finish in the Le Mans 24-Hours endurance race of 1927

and the following year he took second place. Victory came in 1929, and was compounded the year after with another win, the French designer proving beyond doubt that front-wheel-drive was a viable method of transmission.

By 1930, however, Grégoire was moving away from his previous sporting image towards handsome coupé and saloon models, but of which only around 90 were

built. He also changed from S.C.A.P. engines to those of Hotchkiss and Continental, which were competitively priced.

By 1934, car production had ceased, with Grégoire satisfied that he had proved his point. Instead, he put his efforts into marketing the constant-velocity universal joint which he had developed in conjunction with Fenaille.

Top: 1929 12hp model
Above: This 1930 coupé had a 1749cc four-cylinder engine driving the front wheels, a four-speed gearbox and sliding-pillar independent front suspension.

Triumph

Great Britain
1923–1984

The Coventry-based Triumph firm began by making bicycles in 1887. Motor-cycles arrived in 1902 and by the end of World War II the marque had a first-class reputation. Until the early 1930s, the manufacture of motor-cycles remained more important than that of cars, which first appeared in 1923.

The earliest Triumph cars were mainly conventionally engineered and conservatively styled small and medium-sized saloons, although sports tourers arrived in the late 1920s and in 1925 a Triumph became the first British car to have hydraulic brakes. However, Triumph's first noteworthy car was the 1928 Super Seven, a high-quality small family saloon.

More sporting models, some with licence-built Coventry-Climax overhead-valve engines, were introduced at Managing Director Claude Holbrook's behest in the early 1930s. In 1933, Holbrook engaged Donald Healey to oversee development of new models, including the Dolomite, a supercharged straight-eight copied from the Alfa Romeo 8C 2300. But financial difficulties prevented its production or the development of other sporting Triumphs, and the production cars of the era were

Top: 1923 10/20 two-seater
Above: 1932 Super Seven pillarless saloon
Left: 1935 Gloria Southern Cross

high-quality saloons, coupés, and roadsters, mostly with handsome styling to complement their fine engineering. From 1934 there were Glorias; tuned models were known as Gloria-Vitesses and, from 1937, as plain Vitesses. That year, the Dolomite name was applied to a new range of medium-sized models which used the Gloria's chassis design and which eventually replaced both it and the Vitesse.

Too many models and too much competition bankrupted Triumph in 1939, and the company was eventually sold in

1944 to Standard. A 14hp Standard engine powered the post-war 1800cc 'razor-edge' saloon and Roadster, which shared a tubular chassis and independent front suspension, and another Standard engine went into the 1949 Mayflower, a small saloon with razor-edge styling to match that of the 1800, by then re-engined as a 2000.

The Mayflower went in 1953, and for the rest of the decade Triumph flourished as the sporting arm of Standard-Triumph. The 100mph (160km/h) TR2, introduced in 1953, was highly successful both at home and abroad, and led on to a series of open two-seaters which re-established the marque's reputation and culminated in the

Top: 1937 Vitesse drophead coupé
Above: 1939 15hp Dolomite roadster
Left: 1946 1800 roadster
Below: 1950 Renown saloon

Above: 1958 TR3 sports

earned a reputation for unreliability. Other models of the 1960s included the front-wheel-drive 1300 saloon, which failed to meet sales expectations and was

TR6 of 1969. The controversial TR7 of 1975 and its TR8 derivative were designed to meet different requirements and never had the same charisma.

The success of the sports cars persuaded Standard-Triumph to badge all future models as Triumphs. The Triumph Herald accordingly replaced the small Standard saloons in 1959. This was the first Triumph styled by the Italian Michelotti, who would also design the 1963 2000 saloon and the 1970 Stag, a four-seater GT with a V8 engine which

later redeveloped as a rear-wheel-drive range with larger engines. Notable among these was the Dolomite Sprint, a sporting variant introduced in 1972.

Above: 1967 TR4A I.R.S.

Below: The TR2 initiated the famous line of affordable TR sports cars in 1952. Its engine was a 1991cc Standard four-cylinder which gave it a 161km/h (100mph) maximum speed. Sales were brisk, especially in the U.S.A.

Above: 1969 Vitesse 1.6-litre convertible
Above right: 1973 TR6 sports
Right: 1973 Stag sports tourer

Financial difficulties had overtaken the company again in the late 1950s, and in 1960 it had been bought by Leyland Motors. After 1968, Leyland's amalgamation with BMC brought Triumph into direct competition with Rover's big saloons and MG's sports cars. Several projects were cancelled, while the build-quality problems of the TR7 damaged the marque's reputation and probably sealed its fate. The last Triumph was a licence-built Honda Ballade saloon, introduced in 1981 and built until 1984.

The Spitfire was a cheap and popular sports car based on the Herald chassis and running gear. The engine in this early 1960s example was a 67bhp overhead-valve four-cylinder of 1147cc.

Left: 1973 2000 Mk II saloon
Above: 1973 Dolomite Sprint saloon
Below: 1977 TR8 V8 works rally car

TVR

Great Britain
1949 to date

Trevor Wilkinson, from whose Christian name the letters TVR were taken, was born in Blackpool in 1923, becoming an apprentice mechanic at the age of 14. After World War II he set up his own vehicle repair business, Trevcar Motors, and by late 1947 he had gone into partnership with Jack Pickard to form TVR Engineering. It was not until 1953 that he graduated from building one-off specials to a series of cars for general sale, producing 20 in kit or complete form over the next three years.

In 1956 a rolling chassis was bought by American Ray Saidel, who fitted an alloy body and Coventry-Climax engine, renaming the car a Jomar. Successful, Saidel ordered six more.

The same year Bernard Williams, who ran TVR's body suppliers, Grantura Plastics, became a director and the company expanded – too fast, in fact, since it was wound up in 1958. The following year Layton Sports Cars started, although the interruption in supplies spelled the end for Jomar in America.

Above: 1960 1588cc Grantura Mk II

In 1961 two TVR dealers, Keith Aitchison and Brian Hopton, took control and a brief foray into motor sport was attempted. Around that time Trevor Wilkinson left to start manufacturing glassfibre car accessories. Layton gave way to Grantura Plastics in 1962, then Martin Lilley took over three years later. Meanwhile, American dealer Jack Griffith was ordering cars to sell as Griffiths, fitting

Above: 1972 Triumph-engined 2500

Ford V8 engines. This continued until 1965, with TVR selling cars under its own name from 1967.

Martin Lilley pulled out in 1981, having built up the Triumph- and Ford-powered range. Chemical engineer Peter Wheeler then bought the company, initiating the use of the Rover 3.5-litre V8.

In its distinctive wedge-shaped models TVR expanded this engine to 3.9- and 4.2-litres (for the 390i and 420 SEAC models respectively), before returning to a more traditional style for the 2.9-litre Ford V6-powered S roadster, and relaunching the Tuscan name of the early 1970s.

Above: 1982 2.8-litre Tasmin
Below: Tasmin fixed-head coupé

Below: 1986 Rover-engined 350i
Bottom: 1983 TVR Series 2

Top left: 1989 Tuscan race car
Top: 1989 2.9-litre S2C
Above: V8-engined 420 SEAC

Above: 1989 450 SE Convertible

The 1989 TVR S has a two-seater body
made from glassfibre, carbon fibre and
Kevlar on a tubular-steel spaceframe
chassis. The car is powered by a fuel-
injected 3528cc V8 engine developing
225bhp and is claimed to be capable of
250km/h (155mph).

In 1990 TVR showed the new Griffith model, which went into production a year later. It combined stunning good looks with the use of high-tech materials, such as Kevlar and carbonfibre, to keep weight to a minimum. The Griffith was powered by a range of Rover V8-based engines but was later only available with a 5.0-litre unit with 340 horsepower.

Replacing the previous angular V8s was the Chimaera, launched at the Birmingham Motor Show in 1992. It was another fine-looking car with the Rover V8 engine (itself based on a Buick unit) with capacities ranging from 3.9 to 5.0-litres. TVR seemed to be master with this unit and managed to endow it with one of the loveliest exhaust notes ever to have graced a British car.

The Rover engine had its limits, however, and in 1994, TVR launched a new coupé with an engine of its own design and manufacture. The new 75-degree V8 in the Cerbera was a high-tech unit of 4.2 litres, with a flat-plane crankshaft (usually reserved for race engines) and a power output of over 350 horsepower. Performance was earth-shattering with 60mph (100km/h) coming up in around four seconds and a top speed of over 170mph (274km/h).

Above: The Griffith was the first of the new-style TVRs with well-balanced looks and a very powerful V8 engine. This is a late-model Griffith 500, with a 5.0-litre version of the Rover V8

Below: The 400SE was looking very dated by the 1990s but had served the company well through the 1980s

Above: 1997 TVR Cerbera

Below: TVR Chimaera

Vauxhall

Great Britain
1903 to date

The Vauxhall Iron Works Ltd. made marine engines from 1857, but the first Vauxhall car appeared in 1903. In 1904 an improved single-cylinder 6hp model was produced, with wire wheels and a reverse gear. In 1905 the firm moved from London to Luton, and it has been based in the Bedfordshire town ever since.

Above: 1911 Vauxhall Prince Henry　　　*Below: Vauxhall 14/40, 1922 on*

Above: 1904 6hp Vauxhall
Right: 1923 OE Type 30/98

The famous fluted radiator and bonnet, which were to be identifying features of Vauxhalls until the 1950s, were first used in 1906, on the company's 3.3-litre model.

Vauxhall produced a number of cars in the early years, including several three-cylinder models, the 3.3-litre four-cylinder car, and the three-litre (later four-litre) Prince Henry. In addition, a smaller A type, plus D and (six-cylinder) B types were produced. Vauxhalls were successful in motor sport at this time, with 4½-litre Grand Prix models producing some 130bhp.

In 1913 the famous 4½-litre 30/98 was introduced. The car was built until 1928, by which time the car had an

overhead-valve engine and hydraulic brakes. The 30/ 98 tourers were capable of more than 80mph (128km/h) in 1919.

The 14/40 was introduced in 1922, with a detachable cylinder head for its 2.3-litre engine. The car gained a four-speed gearbox from 1925, and a Wilson preselector gearbox was optional in 1927.

Vauxhall came under the control of the American General Motors concern in 1926, after financial problems. The

Above: 1924 Vauxhall Phaeton
Below: 1933 Light Six A type

General Motors-influenced Vauxhall 20/60 was produced from 1927 until 1929, and in the following year the two-litre six-cylinder Cadet was introduced – the first British car to have a synchromesh gearbox. The four-speed 12hp and 14hp Light Sixes replaced the Cadet in 1933. Larger six-cylinder models were produced at the same time.

The advanced Vauxhall 10 of 1937 was built on unitary-construction principles, and also featured torsion-bar front suspension and, in common with other Vauxhalls of the time, overhead valves. The 1203cc engine produced 35bhp and gave lively performance.

Larger Vauxhalls introduced the same year included the massive and luxurious six-cylinder 25 model. Vauxhall Twelve and Fourteen models were also produced, the 1781cc Fourteen producing 48bhp and having a top speed of 70mph (112km/h). Hydraulic brakes were fitted to all Vauxhalls in 1939.

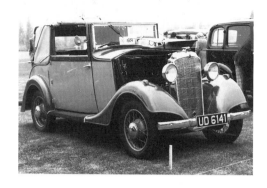

Above: 1934 Light Six ASY 12hp (Tickford)
Below: 1939 Vauxhall 14 J type

The elegant E type Prince Henry Vauxhall 30/98 of 1913 was an impressive performer for its time. Power came from a 4½-litre sidevalve engine. Overhead valves were employed from 1922 (OE type), giving a top speed of 129km/h (80mph).

After World War II, during which Vauxhall produced munitions and the 12-cylinder-engined Churchill tank, the company initially reintroduced its pre-war Ten, Twelve and Fourteen models. However, in 1948 it introduced new models with overhead-valve engines. These were the six-cylinder, 2275cc L Type Velox and the four-cylinder, 1442cc Wyvern, giving 54 and 35bhp respectively.

In 1952 the cars were given new body designs and the shorter-stroke engines now fitted had capacities of 2262cc or 1507cc, producing 65 or 40bhp respectively. In 1955 the models were updated, and a luxury version of the Velox was introduced under the name Cresta.

Above: 1952/3 Velox E type
Below: 1954/5 Cresta

The first Vauxhall Victor – the F Series – was introduced in 1957, with transatlantic styling and a 1508cc overhead-valve engine. In the same year the PA Series Velox and Cresta were introduced, both cars having American-influenced body styling. The engine capacity of these six-cylinder models was increased to 2651cc from August 1960.

Below: 1961 FB Victor Estate

The FB Victor replaced the F Series from September 1961, at first with the 1508cc engine, increased in size to 1595cc from late 1963. The VX4/90 was the twin-carburettor, disc-brake sports version of the Victor saloon, the 1508cc version giving 81bhp, compared with 56bhp from the standard Victor. The six-cylinder Velox and Cresta models were similarly rebodied in late 1962, and designated the PB Series.

Vauxhall's first post-war small car, the HA Viva saloon, was introduced in late 1963, with roomy passenger and luggage accommodation and a lively overhead-valve 1057cc engine developing 44bhp. A Bedford Beagle estate-car version was available from late 1964.

Above: 1970 Viva HC

In October 1964 the 101 Series (PC) Victors appeared with larger, more rounded bodywork. This model was built until it was replaced in October 1967 by the overhead-camshaft 1599cc or 1975cc New Victor (FD). At the same time, new overhead-valve 3294cc Velox and Cresta models were introduced, the luxurious Viscount derivative of the Cresta becoming available in June 1966, and the high-specification Ventora in February 1968. The 3.3-litre engine was optionally available on Victors from May 1968.

In September 1966 the restyled Viva (HB) was introduced, with a 56bhp 1159cc engine. Either two- or four-door bodywork could be specified. SL and De Luxe 90 versions developed 69bhp. Other Vivas included the 1599cc and 1957cc overhead-camshaft models. The HB Viva was replaced by the HC in October 1970, the new car having restyled, larger bodywork and, from September 1971, a 1256cc engine. The HC Viva was also

available with 1759cc or 2279cc overhead-camshaft engines. Derivatives included the Firenza fastback coupé and the Magnum. The Victors were again updated in 1973, and the new models included a 2.3-litre VX4/90.

The 1256cc Chevette range (hatchback/saloon/three-door estate) was introduced in late 1975, and continued in production until 1983.

Above: VX 4/90 of 1973
Below: 1975 Chevette

The Victor's replacement was the Cavalier, launched in October 1975, with up-to-the-minute styling and a choice of 1584cc or 1897cc overhead-camshaft engines; the overhead-valve 1256cc Chevette unit became an optional fitting from late 1977.

Below: 1975 Cavalier 1900 GL Coupé

In the early 1980s many new Vauxhalls featured front-wheel-drive, including the Astra hatchback/estate (1980), the New Cavalier (1981) and the small Nova saloon/hatchback (1983). Large Vauxhalls of this period included the 1979 Carlton (1.8-litre and larger engines), the 1980 2½-litre Viceroy, and the 1979 2.8-litre Royale.

Top: 1980 Astra 1.2 saloon
Above left: 1982 Carlton 2300D Estate

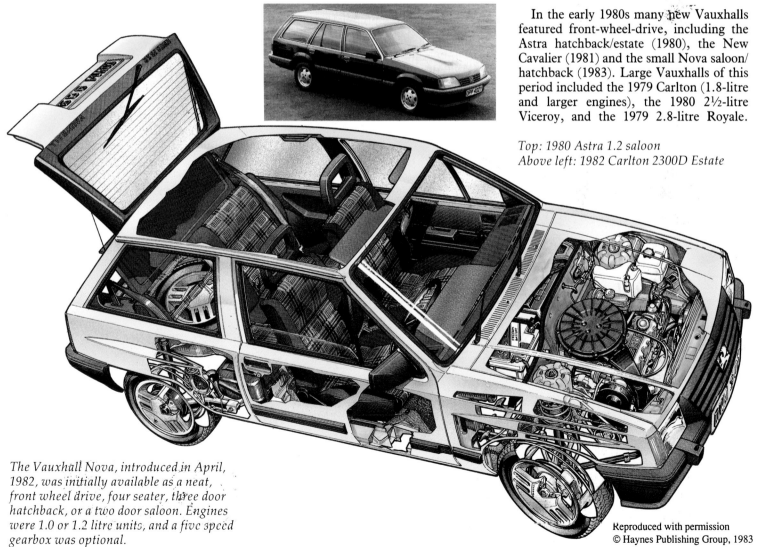

The Vauxhall Nova, introduced in April, 1982, was initially available as a neat, front wheel drive, four seater, three door hatchback, or a two door saloon. Engines were 1.0 or 1.2 litre units, and a five speed gearbox was optional.

The 2.5 and 3.0 litre Senator saloons were introduced, and the Astra range restyled, in October 1984, with the addition of a Belmont saloon version in January 1986.

The Carlton (still rear-wheel-drive) was revised for 1987, as was the Senator for 1988, and in October 1988 a totally new Cavalier range was introduced, to include, from 1989, a four-wheel-drive version.

Right 1989 Calibra Coupé
Below: 1989 Cavalier GSi 2000 16v 4×4

Above and below: 1989 Vauxhall Carlton GSi 3000 24-valve

Bottom left: 1989 Astra GTE 16v on the Lombard RAC International Rally

Above: 1989 Senator 2.5i saloon
Below: 1989 Special Edition Nova 'Sting'

Vauxhall began the 1990s with one of its most outrageous cars ever. The Lotus Carlton was a Carlton that had been heavily breathed on by Lotus to produce a 170mph executive saloon. Flared wheel arches and wide alloy wheels were all that told you that this was no ordinary run-of-the-mill Vauxhall. Unfortunately, adverse press reports questioning the wisdom of a car capable of such high speeds did nothing for sales, and the cars were slow to leave the dealer's forecourt.

By the 1990s, GM had ordained that Vauxhall and Opel products would be almost completely identical, and by the mid-1990s, even the model names were the same in Germany as in the U.K.

The company's Spanish-built super-mini, the Nova, was replaced by a new model in 1993. Now called the Corsa by both Opel and Vauxhall, the new car had rounded styling and was a good seller. A few years later it was falling behind the competition in terms of ride and handling, so Vauxhall employed Lotus engineering to retune the suspension. At the same time a new engine was added to the range: an economical 12-valve three-cylinder, with an output of 54bhp. The result was a car that was back on even terms with its competitors.

The Astra was restyled in 1991 and continued unchanged, apart from a new range of engines in 1995, well into the 1990s. As before, the cabriolet version was built by Bertone. The four-door saloon version was now badged as an Astra, rather than Belmont, as the previous model had been.

Top: 1996 Vauxhall Vectra

Above: 1991 Vauxhall Astra

Right: 1997 Vauxhall Corsa

Below: 1991 Vauxhall Frontera 4x4

Above: *1991 Astra GSi 16-valve*

Below: *1997 Vectra SRi V6 saloon*

Opel also took up the Astra name for the model, dropping the old Kadett label that it had used since the 1930s.

The Calibra, launched in 1989, was a completely new model based on the Cavalier floorpan. The sleek two-door coupé styling proved popular with the buyers and performance was good too. At first the car was fitted with 2.0-litre engines in various states of tune from the 115bhp eight-valve to the 150bhp turbocharged model. In 1993 the model gained Vauxhall's new 2.5-litre V6 which was fitted to the flagship model. This 170bhp unit was beginning to push the car's humble chassis to its limits. Four-wheel-drive versions improved handling, but most were sold in front-wheel-drive form. Another coupé came in 1993. The small Tigra used 1.4- and 1.6-litre engines and had quirky but attractive styling. It was later overshadowed by the superior small coupés of Renault and Ford, the Mégane and Puma.

The Cavalier remained largely unchanged until 1995, but received the new V6 in 1993.

Above left: 1997 Vauxhall Frontera SWB

Above: The Vectra estate came a year after the saloon

Far left: The Vauxhall Monterey was a rebadged Isuzu Trooper

Left: Vauxhall Omega estate

Below: The slippery Calibra coupé

The all-new 1995 model was renamed Vectra and was praised for its smooth styling. The range of engines gave Vauxhall a competitor for the Mondeo at every level, from 1.6 to 2.5 litres. An estate version came later and was launched in 1996.

The Omega was the replacement for the Carlton and Senator models and retained its predecessor's engine and rear wheel drive.

A new departure for the company was a four-wheel-drive leisure vehicle, the Frontera. Designed more with on-road performance in mind, the Frontera wasn't so happy on the rough stuff.

Vauxhall entered the MPV market quite late with the Sintra, launched in 1996. Developed in conjunction with General Motors, it was also built in America.

Above: The Lotus Carlton was the fastest production car with four doors when it was launched in 1989. A top speed of 170mph was deemed excessive by some and adverse press reports didn't help sales

Right: The Vauxhall Sintra was developed in cooperation with parent company, General Motors. Unlike the other Vauxhall/Opel offerings, the Sintra was built in America

Below: The Vauxhall Tigra was launched at the 1993 Frankfurt Motor Show. The large back window was tinted to protect passengers and prevent heat build-up in the cabin

Voisin

France
1919–1939

Famous for his aircraft, Gabriel Voisin built his first experimental car with his brother Charles in 1899, several years before he took to the air. Charles was killed in a road accident in 1912, and their aeroplane manufacturing business halted. After World War I Gabriel set up again, returning to motor vehicles in 1919, having looked at steam power, with an Artaud & Dulfresne design previously turned down by Citroën. Called the Type C1, this employed an engine of 3969cc displacement.

Voisin was as outspoken and eccentric as his cars, disliking chrome, and all things American. He favoured unusual, light-weight, aerodynamic bodywork, often so ugly that it limited sales, although Voisins often attracted rich and famous owners.

By the mid-1920s Voisin was developing Knight double-sleeve-valve engines for his

Above: Voisin C4 Tourer of 1925/6
Below: 1924 C3 (Totnes Motor Museum)

cars, aided by designers Marios Bernard and André Lefèbvre. He spent much money and effort pursuing easy gear changing, trying both Sensaud de Lavaud and Cotal systems on larger, more flexible engines to achieve this.

Belgian Impérias were built under licence in the Issy-les-Moulineaux factory in the early 1930s, when Voisin also produced a number of unusual prototypes, including a front-wheel-drive V8 and an in-line twelve-cylinder engine with the rear two cylinders protruding into the cockpit. This experimentation proved very costly, however, and in 1937 a financial group took over the company.

The Graham-engined model introduced during this period so horrified Voisin that by 1939 he had regained control. He turned to manufacturing a variety of commercial and electrically powered vehicles, and also the aero-engines of Gnome et Rhône, who now owned the company. Voisin remained as president until after World War II, when Gnome et Rhône became part of S.N.E.C.M.A., who discontinued the name by the end of the 1950s.

Gabriel Voisin went on to design the Spanish Biscuter and died in 1973, at the age of 93.

This magnificent Voisin C14 of 1932 was just one example of a range of interesting cars produced by the firm. These included models with V8 and V12 engines, and with distinctive styling. Innovative design was a Voisin feature.

Volkswagen

Germany/West Germany; 1936 to date

Volkswagen – meaning literally 'people's car' – was founded from the ambitions of two totally different characters.

Adolf Hitler was a car enthusiast – although he never learned to drive – who saw motor sport as a way of speeding up technology. He was also intent on having a car for the masses. Austrian-born engineer Dr. Ferdinand Porsche shared the ambition of building a people's car but, having absolutely no interest in politics, had little else in common with Hitler.

Porsche, who was born in 1875, designed his first small car in 1922 – the Austro-Daimler Sascha. Count Sascha Kolowrat privately financed it because Austro-Daimler showed no interest in Porsche's ideas for small cars.

Porsche persevered with his plans for a mass-market car and in 1930 he founded his own design office. The first project was for German manufacturer Wanderer and it heralded the introduction of Porsche's innovative torsion-bar suspension.

However, he wanted to build a larger vehicle with reasonable performance and endurance at an affordable price. A planned deal with motor-cycle manufacturer Zundapp eventually came to nothing. Porsche based his design on Project 12, a car he began working on in 1931, but Zundapp insisted that he use a complex five-cylinder radial engine which was totally contrary to Porsche's objective of simplicity. Zundapp pulled out when the motor-cycle market picked up.

Porsche then found himself a firm ally in Hitler. The latter had plans for an autobahn network and wanted to have a car built which could take advantage of the new roads and sell for under 1000 Deutschmarks. That was less than half the price of the cheapest equivalent vehicle available.

Hitler had heard of Porsche though his Auto Union racing designs and in May 1934 he invited the engineer to submit proposals for a people's car, allowing him a year to complete his presentation.

Porsche saw the price and deadline as daunting propositions. Nevertheless, he decided to try his best. He began work in June 1934 with the reluctant backing of the controlling body of the motor industry – the *Reichsverband der Deutsche Automobilindustrie* (the R.D.A.).

The backing of other manufacturers was so poor, however, that Porsche's first three prototypes were built in his own garage. Indeed, many manufacturers openly admitted their opposition to the engineer's efforts, notably Opel which was then producing Germany's cheapest 'real' car.

Porsche initially believed that the engine had to be a two-stroke unit to meet the price target, but the first prototype, completed in October 1936, had a low-compression, air-cooled, flat-four, four-stroke engine of 985cc.

Above: Prototype VW3 and VW30, 1936–7

Vast mileages were covered over the next two months in testing the first three prototypes. Many problems were encountered such as torsion bars breaking and engines having short lives. But Hitler was apparently satisfied and in February 1937 told the R.D.A. that the project must have full backing.

Three months later, the *Gesellschaft für Vorbereitung des Deutschen Volkswagens GmbH* (the association for the manufacture of the German people's car) was founded. It was state-backed to the tune of 480,000 Deutschmarks.

A batch of 30 prototypes was built and exhaustively tested, mostly by military drivers. Meanwhile, Porsche twice visited the U.S.A. to study modern mass-production methods.

Hitler made the next move and laid the foundation stone at the factory at Fallersleben, near Hanover, in May 1938. Volkswagenwerk GmbH was registered to produce the cars in October 1938 and Hitler decreed that a town should be built especially for the workers. It was known as Kraft durch Freude Stadt. The name was chosen after the Strength through Joy movement which Hitler used to promote the project.

Hitler announced that the new car would be called the KdF-wagen, much to Porsche's dismay, and that it was to be financed by advance-purchase payments and available through a stamp-saving scheme run by a central agency. Over 350,000 accounts were opened before the outbreak of World War II.

Production started in April 1939, but only 210 KdF-wagens were built before the factory turned its attentions to the war effort. And despite Hitler's odd choice of its name, the car had already become known as the Beetle.

The plant was devastated by bombing and eventually passed to British military control at the end of the war. The British renamed KdF Stadt as Wolfsburg in May 1945 and began a rebuilding programme. Both the plant and the Beetle were offered to other countries – but none showed an interest.

Possibly the only person to recognize the Beetle's potential was Major Ivan Hirst, the British officer in charge. Under his command, production resumed in August 1945, and 1,785 Volkswagens were built by the end of the year, all for the services. The next year saw a vast expansion and more than 10,000 were made, mostly with 1131cc engines.

Above: 1947 export-specification Beetle

The company was handed back to Germany in January 1948 and Hirst appointed Heinrich Nordhoff as general manager.

Nordhoff, a banker's son who had worked for Opel and B.M.W. and was well-versed in American mass-production methods, was a firm believer in exporting, and by 1948 about a quarter of all Beetles went abroad. Nordhoff broke new ground the following year when two cars were exported to the United States – the first of several million.

Porsche had been released from internment by this time and was engaged as an engineering consultant. He received royalties on every Beetle made and the rewards were great enough for him to carry on and build the famous sports cars which bear his name.

The American market quickly expanded, and within a decade half of the cars made were sold there.

July 1949 saw the introduction of a better-equipped export Beetle and the Karmann four-seater cabriolet was introduced at the same time. This latter model went on until early 1979, during which time about 330,000 were built. The Beetle's mechanicals were also used for the March 1950 Transporter van.

Hitler's stamp scheme had left Nordhoff with an expensive legacy from the pre-war years. Many investors asked for discounts and claims cases were heard in courts for many years, some as late as the 1960s.

Partial discounts were eventually given on more than 120,000 cars.

During the 1950s, several overseas VW offshoots were set up including Volkswagen do Brasil, Volkswagen Australia, Volkswagen France and Volkswagen America.

In 1954, the Germans introduced a larger 1192cc engine and continued to improve the Beetle both cosmetically and mechanically. And one year later VW took its relationship with coachbuilder Karmann further by asking it to build the Karmann Ghia Type 1, a sporty-looking coupé.

There was some confusion over who actually owned Volkswagen – national or local government – so the company was reorganized as Volkswagenwerk GmbH and shares were offered to the public. They bought 60 per cent with the rest going to national and local government.

The 1500 saloon complemented the Beetle in 1961 and its 1493cc flat-four

Top right: 1960 U.K.-specification Beetle
Centre right: Rallying Type 3 411 saloon
Right: 1965 1600cc Variant saloon

The Beetle changed remarkably little during its long production life. Most numerous was the 1200, built from 1960 to 1978 and featuring a 1192cc version of the familiar overhead-valve flat four engine.

engine was used in the Karmann-Ghia coupé.

Production of Volkswagens reached five million by December 1961 and it subsequently never fell below one million a year. In 1971 the figure topped no less than two million. During the 1960s other options were offered such as the Variant estate, the TL fastback and the unitary-construction 411 saloon and estate of 1969. But the Beetle still ruled the roost. From 1965, Volkswagen was also building certain Audi models since taking over Auto-Union from Daimler-Benz.

Nordhoff died in April 1969, shortly before he had planned to retire, and his successor Kurt Lotz almost immediately began to face problems. Doubts were growing about the Beetle's future and Volkswagen had been overtaken as Europe's most prolific car-maker by Fiat.

Volkswagen took over N.S.U. in 1969 and amalgamated it with Audi to form N.S.U. Auto Union AG. The N.S.U. K70 prototype, using a derivative of the Wankel-engined RO80, was launched as the Volkswagen K70 in 1971.

It was a break with tradition, being the first front-engined, water-cooled Volkswagen. But it did little to impress the public and never sold in great numbers.

However, Volkswagen had reason to celebrate in February 1972 when a total of 15,007,034 Beetles had been built, surpassing the Ford Model T's production record (the last German-built Beetle was a cabriolet made in April 1979. The 20

Below: Water-cooled 1972 K70 L
Centre: 1972 411 LE saloon
Bottom: Type 1 Karmann Ghia, c. 1972

Above: 1968 1300cc Beetle Cabriolet
Below: 1969/70 Type 3 estate car

Above: The 411 version of the Type 3 chassis
Below: Type 3 fastback c. 1969/70

millionth Beetle left the production line in Mexico in May 1981).

But the company could not afford to become complacent because Opel overtook it as Germany's leading manufacturer in 1971. As popular and durable as the Beetle was, it needed a replacement.

The first new-generation Volkswagen was the front-wheel-drive Passat, a derivative of the Audi 80, and it came in 1973. The firm was in danger of folding in 1974 but was mainly saved by the Giugiaro-styled Golf and Scirocco – both featured front-wheel drive and used the same running gear.

Top left: 1973 two-door Passat
Far right: Four-door 1973 Type 4 saloon
Right: 1974 Giugiaro-designed Scirocco

Below: The original Golf was introduced in 1974. In its most basic form it featured a 1093cc overhead-camshaft engine and soon became one of the most popular small hatchbacks in the world. U.S.-built Golfs were given the name Rabbit, along with slightly different trim and lights.

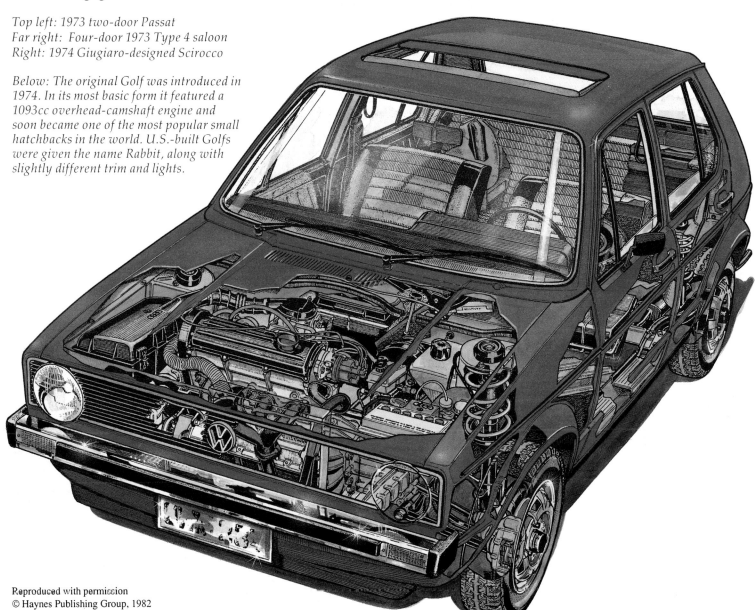

The smaller Polo hatchback came in 1975 and then its 'three-box' derivative the Derby. The Jetta – a three-box Golf – followed in 1979.

The Americans soon took to the Golf – they know it as the Rabbit – and a production plant was opened at New Stanton, Pennsylvania.

Diesel Golfs and Passats were introduced to the range and Volkswagen did much for its image with the 110bhp fuel-injected Golf GTi which had been introduced in 1976.

Above: 1975 Polo hatchback
Above right: 1978/9 Scirocco GLi sports coupé
Right: 1979/80 Jetta, the Mk 1 Golf with a boot

Below: The Mk 1 Golf GTI was available in the U.K. from 1979, but initially only in left-hand-drive form. With a 1600cc fuel-injected engine developing 110bhp, the car was capable of around 183km/h (114mph) and quickly became a true trend-setter.

The 35 millionth Volkswagen rolled off the production line in June 1979 – a German-built Golf.

Volkswagen branched out and agreed for Passats and Polos to be built under licence by SEAT of Spain in 1953. And in 1982, Volkswagen signed an agreement with the Chinese government to have the Santana – a notchback version of the Passat – built at the Shanghai Motor Works. The Santana was also built under licence by Nissan in Japan.

Right: 1982 Polo Classic GL saloon
Below right: Restyled Scirocco for 1982
Below: Polo C three-door hatchback
Bottom: Limited-edition 1982 Scirocco Scala

Below: 1981 Volkswagen Auto 2000 development vehicle. Designed for maximum efficiency, it has a lightweight body, a drag coefficient of 0.25 and is designed to be powered by either a supercharged 1050cc petrol engine or a 1191cc diesel.

Above: 1981 Volkswagen Santana GX four-door saloon

Below: 1983 Passat five-door hatchback

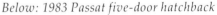

Despite financial losses in the face of increasing competition, Volkswagen continued introducing new models with a sporting bias. They included the fleet-footed 16-valve Scirocco which could comfortably top 209km/h (130mph). The 16-valve engine became available in the GTi by mid-1985, making the car the definitive hatchback by which all the others were judged. And the rallying-inspired Golf Syncro, introduced in 1988, elevated roadholding levels further with permanent four-wheel drive.

In 1989 VW replace the Scirocco with

Below: The Mk 2 Jetta inherited the general front-end appearance of the mechanically similar Mk 2 Golf. Specifications ranged from the 150km/h (93mph) 1272cc C up to the 1.8-litre 112bhp fuel-injected unit used in the 1986 Jetta GT. A 16-valve engine followed in 1988.

another front-wheel-drive 2+2-seater coupé, the Corrado. This is offered with the Golf's 1.8-litre 16-valve four-cylinder engine, or an eight-valve 1.8-litre unit with supercharging. The latter makes 136bhp, taking the Corrado onto territory which in the 1980s had belonged to Porsches – a far cry from the humble Beetle.

*Above: 1984 MK 2 Golf GL
Below: 1988/89 4wd Golf Syncro*

*Above: 1050cc Polo C saloon of 1985
Below: 1990 Passat GT 16V saloon*

Below: 1988 Polo Ranger hatchback

*Above: 1990 Corrado 16V sports coupé
Below: Catalyst-equipped Polo for 1990*

*Above: 1990 five-door Golf GL
Bottom right: 1990 Golf GTI Convertible*

*Above: Rallye Golf G60 of 1990
Below: 1990-specification Scirocco GTII*

The Polo was updated in 1990 with a face-lift, but was replaced with a truly new model in 1994. By this time, Seat was building all Polos. Despite the car's relative lack of flair compared with its other European super-mini rivals, it continued to sell well to those who prized the VW badge and the build quality and reliability that went with it. It was praised as having real 'big car feel' and performance became more competitive with the arrival of the 16-valve engine.

A joint venture with Ford provided a people carrier for the Volkswagen range. The Sharan had more kudos than the Ford-badged Galaxy, but the two vehicles were identical apart from the different badging and trim packages.

The Passat was completely updated in 1988, with new aerodynamic styling and continued, with a few minor face-lifts, until it was replaced again in 1996. The 1996 car was completely new. It had more appealing, less dowdy styling than its predecessor, as well as a whole new range of engines, including a rather unusual V5.

The Jetta disappeared with the Mk2 Golf and was replaced by the Vento. Unlike its

Left: Volkswagen's new Beetle. In the mid-1990s Volkswagen decided to create a modern-day Beetle. At first it was just a concept car, but the designers persisted and it started to look as though it would reach production. It used the Volkswagen Golf platform and engines. That means a front-mounted engine and front-wheel-drive

Below: The Volkswagen Sharan was the result of a collaboration with Ford. There were essentially three versions of the same car: the Sharan, the Ford Galaxy and the Seat Alhambra. By collaborating in this way, both Ford and the Volswagen group managed to keep development costs to a minimum when entering the MPV market

Above: Mk3 Golf GTi was bigger and slower than its predecessor

Below: The Vento also came with the VR6 engine

predecessor, the Vento was more of a car in its own right and less of a Golf with a boot. Unfortunately, like the Jetta, the Vento wasn't a huge sales success but remained in the VW range.

In 1996, Volkswagen Group was the fourth largest car manufacturer in the world and the biggest in Europe behind the General Motors Group, the Ford empire and the Japanese giants, Toyota having built a total of 3,537,016 vehicles at all its manufacturing plants around the world, of which approximately 2.5 million were Volkswagen-badged. With its empire growing all the time, the company looked set to begin moving up the rankings.

Left: Unlike previous Volkswagen Golfs, the Mk3 model was available in estate form

Below: The Mk3 Passat was launched in 1997

Volkswagen's fine cars during the 1980s gave the company such an image boost that it seemed nothing could stop it. The Golf had become a legend in its own time and continued to sell well. A new Mk3 version was launched in 1991. This time, the GTi was no longer the top of the range. The new king of the Golfs was the VR6 which was a 170bhp version of Volkswagen's new narrow-angle V6. The same 2.8-litre engine was also fitted to the Corrado. The GTi remained as popular as ever, and comfortably outsold the VR6. It seemed that people were now buying for the GTi badge rather than ultimate performance. The turbodiesel model wasn't short of performance either, with a top speed of over 110mph (177km/h).

VW's worldwide approach saw huge numbers of cars being produced. In 1993, there were more than a million Golfs built in VW's factories in Germany, Belgium, Yugoslavia, Mexico and South Africa. The group's 1991 total of 3.3 million vehicles was a 56 per cent increase over figures from the previous 10 years. A 4-million total was estimated for the turn of the century.

Above: The Polo saloon

Below: Polo five-door hatchback

Above: Mk3 Golf Cabriolet

Below: The Golf VR6 was faster than the GTi

VW/SEAT

To bring the Volkswagen story fully up to date, however, it is necessary to turn to the cosmopolitan mixture of Italian styling, German engineering and Spanish manufacturing expertise that has resulted in the current SEAT range of vehicles.

For over 30 years SEAT had been building Fiat cars under licence in Spain (as well as Volkswagens themselves, of course). In 1980 Fiat terminated this arrangement, forcing SEAT either to close or to develop its own product. The company chose the latter and, in only four years, developed the Ibiza hatchback.

So impressed was Volkswagen with this success that in 1986 it acquired 75 per cent of SEAT from the Spanish government and, during 1990, assumed full control – with a commitment to developing a new model range, new manufacturing facilities and a research establishment.

Top right: Three-door Ibiza 1.5 GLX
Right: Marbella 850 similar to Fiat Panda
Below: 1960 SEAT 600

Right: 1.2-litre Malaga saloon
Below: 1990 Terra Vista light commercial

Above: Ibiza SXi

Below: 1990 Limited-edition Marbella 'Red'

Soon SEAT was building all of Volkswagen's Polos and had some new models of its own. The new Ibiza, first shown at the Barcelona Salon in 1993, was the first example of how Volkswagen was going to improve the Spanish company's product range. Ultra-modern styling, fine build quality and a range of Volkswagen engines gave SEAT a car that attracted a welcome market of new buyers who'd never even heard of the company before. Later in the 1990s, the company added a GTi to the range with the 8-valve VW Golf GTi engine. It was swiftly followed by the more powerful 16-valve engine and a special-edition model called the Cupra, to celebrate the car's Championship win in Group A rallying in 1996. A saloon version, the Cordoba was launched a year later.

SEAT's medium-sized offering was the Toledo four-door hatchback, which also used Volkswagen and Audi power units. Strangely, and despite being entirely owned by Volkswagen, SEAT continued to build the Marbella, the company's version of the Fiat Panda that it had built since 1982. At the other end of the range, SEAT stuck its badge on the VW/Ford MPV, and called it the Alhambra.

Below: 1997 SEAT Toledo SE

Right: SEAT Cordoba 1.4

A new Volkswagen-based small car came in 1997. The Arosa was a three-door super-mini with Volkswagen Polo engine. Designed to compete with Ford's Ka, the Arosa was the first SEAT-badged car to be built at Volkswagen's Wolfsburg factory.

SEAT had built themselves a $2 billion

Top: Base-model Ibiza with 1.0-litre engine
Below: 1997 SEAT Arosa
Bottom: SEAT Alhambra

Above: The SEAT range in 1997. Every model was Volkswagen-based

Right: The SEAT Ibiza Cupra Sport was a special edition to celebrate the car's 1996 victory in Group A of the World Rally Championship

new factory at Martorell, near Barcelona, and its daily production potential of 1200 Ibizas was meant to help SEAT achieve annual rates of over 800,000 cars, 75 per cent of them for export.

Unfortunately 1992 and 1993 were not good years and Volkswagen had to provide emergency aid of over £900 million to keep SEAT afloat. In 1994, to make up for further losses, SEAT was forced to sell its Pamplona plant for $160 million and its commercial operations for $65 million.

Volvo

Sweden
1927 to date

The company was founded by Assar Gabrielsson and Gustav Larson, allegedly during a meal consisting of crayfish, in 1924. Their first car, the 1944cc Jakob, was in production by 1927.

Born in 1891, Gabrielsson had studied economics, and was sales manager for the Swedish bearings company SKF, at the time he joined up with Larson. The latter was four years older, and had worked for automotive company White and Poppe in Coventry, England, from 1911 to 1913, before joining SKF in 1917. In 1920 he left and was working as technical manager for AB Galco when he was reunited with Gabrielsson.

The scheme was to build a vehicle more suited to the Scandinavian climate than were U.S. imports, utilizing high-quality Swedish steel and bought-in components. Gabrielsson financed the completion of ten prototypes, with bodies styled by Swedish artist Helmer Mas-Olle. Marine engineers Pentaverken built and supplied the engines, and SKF was sufficiently impressed to fund the production run of the first thousand cars, built at Lundby, near Gothenburg, from 1927. SKF also allowed the partners to use one of the company's patented names: AB Volvo, which derives from the Latin 'I roll', with its obvious connotations of bearings in action.

The company had planned to build 500 cabriolets and 500 saloons but, in the event, only 205 of the steel-bodied open cars were produced, compared with 721 of the closed fabric-bodied PV4 models. In 1929 a three-litre straight-six was

Volvo OV4 1927

Left: Debutante Volvo, the OV4 of 1927
Above: PV651s were built from 1929–1934

Below: Launched in January 1960, the P1800 sports coupé was powered by a 115bhp four-cylinder engine. Initial production was carried out in Great Britain; bodies were made at the Pressed Steel plant at Linwood, and the cars were assembled by Jensen. An estate-car derivative, the P1800ES, continued to be made until 1973.

*Above: The U.S.-influenced PV36
'Carioca', a stylish mid-'30s model
Right: The PV53, produced in 1938–1945
Below right: P120 series lasted 14 years*

introduced, designated the PV650, and this enjoyed an eight-year production run until 1937, during which time there were capacity increases to 3.2 and 3.6 litres, with a few longer-wheelbase chassis made for specialist coachbuilders. The PV36 of 1936 bore a similarity to the Chrysler Airflow.

Concurrently Volvo was also producing 1½-ton trucks, from 1928, and a range of taxis known as TRs, based on the PV4. The trucks actually outsold the cars until World War II.

By 1932, the company was in profit and operating from its own factory; output was well over 900 cars a year, although demand slackened slightly due to economic factors during the mid-1930s. SKF relinquished control of Volvo with a stock flotation in 1935, and at the same time Volvo took over Pentaverken which, as AB Penta, became in 1949 the marine-engineering division of Volvo.

Sweden's neutrality allowed Volvo to maintain production during World War II, although the production figure of 2,834 cars in 1939 fell back to a low of 99 in 1942. The 50,000th Volvo was a truck, built in 1941.

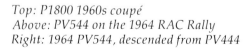

Top: P1800 1960s coupé
Above: PV544 on the 1964 RAC Rally
Right: 1964 PV544, descended from PV444

Volvo's first post-war car was the stylish PV444, which had been conceived in 1942 and featured independent front suspension and coil springs at the rear. This proved an important model in that it gained Volvo a foothold in the U.S.A. For the first time, cars were outselling trucks, prompting a major investment programme which saw several derivatives of the PV444 produced, including estates and light commercials. Some 500,000 units were made, including the PV544 development, which was built until 1965, and the PV210 estate which was in production until 1969.

Not noted for adventurous styling, Volvo came out with a short run of 67 glassfibre sports cars, based on the PV444, and styled in the U.S.A. in 1955 by Glaspar, of Kaiser Darrin fame. The project was squashed when the Suez crisis threatened vehicular indulgence.

The company's next venture into the world of the semi-exotic was to be the P1800 coupé of 1961, styled initially by Italian coachbuilders Ghia and finished off by Frua. To start with, bodies were made by the British firm of Pressed Steel after Karmann pulled out, and the vehicles were assembled by Jensen at West Bromwich, near Birmingham. However, Volvo found sufficient capacity and resources to shift production to Sweden in 1963, where the car continued to be made until 1973 in the form of a sporting estate car called the P1800ES. The P1800 won lasting fame as the car driven by actor Roger Moore in film adaptations of *The Saint* detective stories, and the 115bhp engine was also used in Facellia and Marcos sports cars.

Gabrielsson retired in 1956, although he remained chairman until his death in 1962. Larson died in 1968, but the pair had already initiated development of the P120 series prior to Gabrielsson's retirement. The 121 saloon was known as the Amazon, but only marketed with this nomenclature in Sweden because of a prior claim to the name by German motor-cycle manufacturers Kreidler.

A new factory was built with Swedish Government backing at Torslanda, and opened by King Gustav Adolf in 1964. Volvo had already started to build its cars in Canada and Belgium. The millionth car was an Amazon, in 1966, and in the same year the 140 series was announced. The six-cylinder 164 appeared in 1968 and, by 1970, the Amazon was phased out. The

Top: Fast, sporting Volvo 132S 'Amazon'
Above: 1971 Volvo 164 with 6 cylinders

Above: By 1974, 144GL had huge bumpers
Below: Capacious 1970s 145 estate

144s were updated to become 240s in 1974, and a further face-lift produced the 244 saloons and 245 estates, which also now include diesel and turbocharged options. The 260 series of 1974 was fitted with the PRV 2.7-litre V6 engine, a unit developed jointly by a consortium of Peugeot, Renault and Volvo.

By 1983, output had reached five million cars, and included the 760 series, launched in 1982. These somewhat angular cars were powered by 2.8-litre V6 diesels from VW, or turbocharged 2.3-litre fours, and a spacious estate appeared in 1985.

The same year's Geneva motor show also saw the launch of a Bertone-designed 780 coupé, based on the 760 floorpan. This was hardly a sports model, although it did preface the introduction in 1986 of the Volvo 480ES, a front-wheel-drive hatchback which was conceptually rather similar to the P1800ES. The 480 used a 1.7-litre Renault engine, and was built in the Netherlands at the Volvo BV plant.

This particular factory came into Volvo ownership when the company acquired a 75 per cent interest in DAF's car division. Volvo had started negotiations with DAF as early as 1969, and gained its controlling

interest after a series of financial moves. In 1976, DAF's four-cylinder Variomatic-transmission 66 model became a Volvo, heralding the introduction of the rather mundane 340 series. By 1981, the Dutch government had invested sufficient capital in the company to reduce Volvo's stake to a 30 per cent share.

Volvo's other interests range from trucks and buses, aero-engines and boats to food, oil and mineral exploration, and the company is particularly active in developing its own brand of advanced vehicle technology, which includes electronic traction control, four-wheel steering and heated steering wheels.

Above : 6-cylinder power for 164 of 1974

Below: The Volvo 244 was introduced in 1974, an updated version of the familiar 140 series. This model helped consolidate Volvo's reputation for building robust vehicles, and the range was expanded to include diesel and turbocharged models.

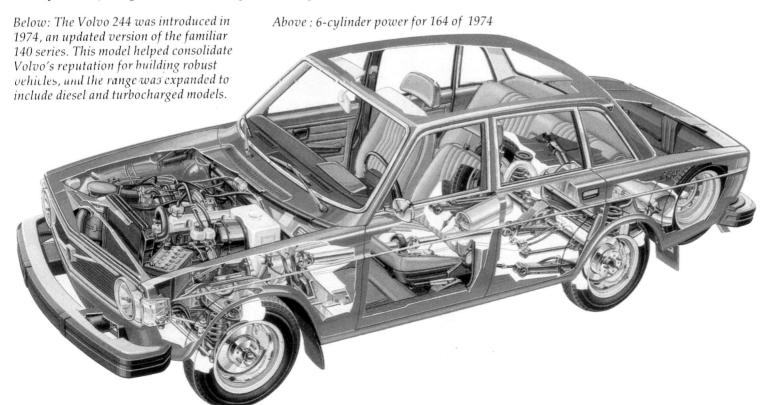

GJU 750

Above: Volvo's 2-litre 240 Saloon

Above: 1990 workhorse: the 240 Estate

Above: The popular Volvo 340

Above: The spacious and economical 740

Below: 16-valve turbo 740 Estate

Above: Mid-range saloon, the 440 of 1989

Above: The 480ES with a 1721cc engine

Left: Facelifted 760 Estate of 1990
Above: Most luxurious was the 760 Saloon

Above: Volvo S70, 1997

Below: The 960 replacement, the S90

As Volvo started the 1990s, much speculation surrounded it regarding a possible deal with Renault. The deal was to take advantage of economies of scale and maximize the benefits of joint activities in purchasing, with a target of raising the number of shared parts suppliers, and therefore shared components, in order to reduce product costs. The planned link would have put the Renault-Volvo group as the third largest manufacturer in Europe with a 12.3 per cent market share. In the event, the link-up never took place.

Profits were fluctuating in the early nineties with a $120 million profit in 1991 and a $520 million loss in 1992. This was in spite of an increase in sales in 1992 which had come about thanks to the launch of the 850.

The 850 was a big departure for Volvo. Unlike its previous larger cars, the 850 was front-wheel-drive and used an all-new five-cylinder engine. Top of the range was the 850 T5 with a turbocharged 2.3-litre engine. Performance was astounding, and surprised many drivers. The car still had Volvo's tradi-

Above: Volvo V90 estate

Below: 1997 Volvo S40

tional angular styling, albeit slightly updated, but had the performance of a real sports car. Volvo entered the T5 estate in the British Touring Car Championship where it competed very successfully against much sportier-looking cars.

The losses were turned around in 1995, helped partly when Sweden, along with Finland and Austria, joined the European Union. Within the first six months following this event, Volvo's sales were up by 14 per cent in a market which had increased by just 1.2 per cent; in Japan, where overall sales increased by 5.5 per cent, Volvo sold 25 per cent more cars, and in Europe as a whole, where total sales were up only 1.4 per cent, Volvo sales increased by 11 per cent. Volvo executives attributed the success to the company's return to concentrating on Europe, after 30 years of spreading itself too widely and too thinly across the world.

By the late 1990s, Volvo had dropped the three-figure model designations and extended its range. The biggest shock was a Volvo with curves. The S40/V40 range was the result of a joint venture with Mitsubishi. The styling of the car was much more up to date than its predecessor, the 440, and it was hoped to help sales in south-east Asian markets.

The 850, which had done so much for

Volvo by adding a degree of excitement to the company's previously dull image, was replaced in 1996. The new car, designated S70 for the saloon and V70 for the estate version, also brought new innovation to the company with the four-wheel-drive system fitted to certain models.

Another big surprise was the launch of new convertible and coupé models. Called the C70, the new coupé followed in the foot-

steps of its spiritual predecessor, the P1800 coupé, by appearing as the Saint's stylish wheels in a Hollywood film remake of the original series.

Above: 1997 Volvo V40

Below: 1997 Volvo S70

Above: The estate version of the S70, the V70

Below: The curvaceous C70 Coupé

White

U.S.A.
1900–1918

Rollin H. White was the son of Thomas H. White, whose White Manufacturing Co. of Cleveland, Ohio, produced a number of articles from sewing machines to roller skates. Rollin built his first steam-powered car, a simple machine with a floor-mounted single-cylinder engine, in 1900. This proved popular, with just under 200 sold in 1901, and two years later a two-cylinder model arrived.

Right: 1906 White Steamer

Below: Early steam-powered Whites were built on an armoured wooden frame, using a front-mounted engine with a condenser in the conventional radiator position. By 1905 a two-speed rear axle was standard.

By 1906 production was running at 1,500 a year. The steam cars were expensive, but pulled well and were noted for reliability. They performed respectably in the Glidden Tours, and specials, like the underslung-frame Whistling Billy of Webb Jay, recorded a speed of 74.04mph (119.15km/h) over a mile. Roosevelt even drove one while in office at the White House.

By 1911 the steamers had given way to petrol-engined models, White having bought the Waltham Manufacturing company in order to do so. Both cars and commercials were built by the company, the latter from 1901.

In 1914 Rollin left White to set up on his own, going on to build the Rollin car during the early 1920s, and the company was reformed as the White Motor Co. During the war years car production declined, to the point where, after 1918, they were made to special order only.

The company then concentrated entirely on commercial vehicles. White was taken over briefly by Studebaker in the early 1930s, then went independent again to build large numbers of military vehicles during World War II. During the 1950s it acquired Sterling, Autocar, Reo and Diamond T, only to sell off most of its holdings during financial problems in the 1970s. White finally went bankrupt in 1980 and was sold to a variety of buyers, including Volvo.

Above: 1905 steam-powered limousine

Above: This 1911 car had a petrol engine

Below: 2.4-litre Rollin-bodied White

Below: 'Town car' on White 158 chassis

Willys

U.S.A.
1907–1963

When John North Willys bought the financially troubled Standard Wheel Company in 1907, he rapidly upgraded production from single- and twin-cylinder runabouts to four-cylinder models and to sixes after 1909. That year, the name Overland appeared and, from 1910, the Willys name was dropped. After 1908, all production was centred on Toledo, Ohio.

By 1914, Overland was a best-selling make, and the following year was second only to Ford in sales. Overland models were supplemented after 1914 by sleeve-valve cars under the Willys-Knight name. A V8 Overland arrived in 1917, but after 1919 only sidevalve fours were available until 1925, when sixes again appeared in both Overland and Willys-Knight ranges.

Peak sales were achieved in 1929, but the Depression caused a sales slump. The four-cylinder models were dropped in 1931, and the Willys-Knight sleeve-valve models died out a year later. From 1933 to 1936, the company was in receivership, and its only product was the low-cost Model 77, marketed as a Willys until 1939, when the Overland name was revived.

The military Jeep, built in huge numbers after 1941, used the engine developed for the 1941 Americar saloons. Though wartime Jeep production was shared with Ford, Willys had sole rights after 1945 and developed a whole range of civilian variants, the descendants of which are still in production. Jeeps alone were made until 1952, when the Aero saloons were introduced. A year later, the company was bought by Kaiser, but the Aero models continued until 1957. Thereafter, U.S. production was only of Jeeps, but some cars were made under the Willys-Overland name in Brazil until 1967. Elsewhere, the Willys name died out in 1963 when the company's name was changed to the Kaiser-Jeep Corporation.

Right: 1955 Bermuda two-door hardtop

Above: 1920 Willys Overland   *Below: 1929 Willys-Knight Great Six*

Above: 1968 Jeep Jeepster Commando

Above left: 1961 Jeep Utility Wagon

The 1926 Willys-Overland Whippet was a successful model with a 2.2-litre sidevalve four-cylinder engine.

Winton

U.S.A.
1897–1924

Alexander Winton was a bicycle maker who first experimented with cars in 1897. Of Scottish birth, he founded the Winton Motor Carriage Co. in Cleveland, Ohio, that year, producing his first vehicle for sale, a two-seater, single-cylinder buggy, in 1898. Early owners included the Packard brothers, who set up their own motor manufacturing business with two former Winton employees.

By the turn of the century Winton was the largest American petrol-driven car producer and Alexander Winton had also begun to take part in competition. His first try was an unsuccessful attempt in the first Gordon Bennett Cup event with a single-cylinder vehicle of 3.8 litres.

A new factory was purchased in 1902, and a new two-cylinder model launched. The following year Winton tried again in racing, with two Bullet cars, an 8.5-litre

The 17B Touring of 1911 was the product of the Winton decision to go for the luxury car market exclusively.

four-cylinder vehicle and a four-litre eight-cylinder version, which were driven by Percy Owen and by Winton himself. These were entered in the Gordon Bennett Cup race, but neither completed the event. Both cars, however, went on to small successes in sprint racing.

Four-cylinder-engined cars were offered commercially from 1904, but four years later Winton turned exclusively to luxury sixes, selling a total of 1,200 cars in 1909. By 1915 less-expensive vehicles were offered, forming the basis of Winton's range up to 1920, during which time few changes were implemented.

A change of direction came in 1912 when Winton began making marine diesel engines and stationary machines through the newly formed Winton Gas Engine Manufacturing Co. By 1923 car production had declined considerably and Winton's shareholders chose to concentrate on the diesel-engine side of the business, which eventually became part of General Motors Cleveland Division in 1930. The final Winton car was built in 1924.

Opposite top: One of the first – an 1899 model
Above: The 1903 Winton Bullet racing car
Below: A 1920 Winton Six Model 24 French Limousine

Wolseley

Great Britain
1896–1975

The first Wolseley was a single-cylinder, two-horsepower three-wheeler, made by the company's General Manager, Herbert Austin, in 1896. The first four-wheeled Wolseley appeared in 1899, a 3½-horsepower model. In 1901 tiller steering gave way to a wheel, and the single-cylinder car (now 5hp) was joined by a 2.6-litre 10hp model plus a special-order four-cylinder, five-speed racing machine. The following year a 5.2-litre model was introduced, also with four cylinders.

The famous racing Wolseley Beetles, with flat four-cylinder 11.9hp engines, were highly successful during 1904 and 1905, in which year Austin left Wolseley to form his own company.

J. D. Siddeley designed a 3.3-litre, four-cylinder Wolseley-Siddeley, 1906 versions featuring overhead inlet valves.

Above: 1904 Wolseley 24hp Wagonette with a distinctive wraparound radiator and chain drive

Below: The Wolseley 16/20 became a popular model in the years just prior to World War I. This is a 1911 example, with open bodywork. Dual ignition and air pressure fuel feed were features of 1913 16/20 models.

A wide range of models was produced until 1910, by which time Siddeley had left to join the Deasy company. Wolseleys continued to be built, and by the start of World War I, two bevel-drive six-cylinder models, of 24/30 and 30/40hp, were on offer.

After the war, during which the company had built Hispano-Suiza aircraft engines, Wolseley produced overhead-camshaft-engined models, as well as a sidevalve six-cylinder car of 3.9-litres capacity, made until 1927.

Wolseleys were built in 7, 10 (later, 11/22) and 15hp form during the 1920s, the 15hp model being replaced by a sidevalve 16/35 in 1925. Later Wolseley models were all to feature overhead-camshaft or overhead-valve engines.

Sir William Morris (Lord Nuffield) acquired the bankrupt Wolseley company

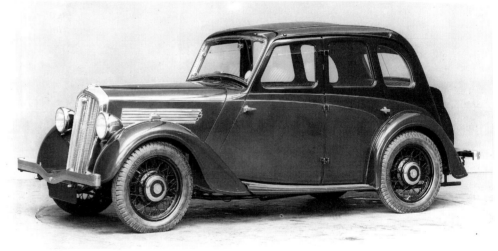

Top: 1910 50hp Limousine
Above: 1923 10hp Doctor's Coupé
Right: 1935 Wolseley 10 saloon
Below: 1937 18hp Wolseley in wartime

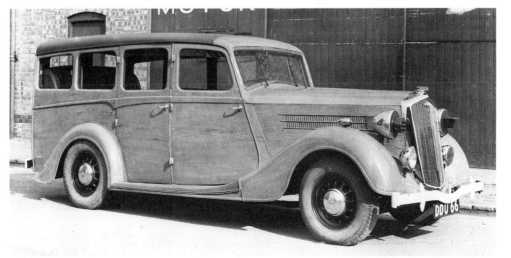

in 1927, and one of the interesting cars to emerge under the new management was the 1929 21/60, a hydraulically braked six-cylinder model which closely resembled the Morris Isis.

In 1930 Wolseley introduced the famous six-cylinder 1300cc Hornet, a fast, comfortable small saloon, based on the Morris Minor. Sports and special-bodied versions proved popular.

Larger models of the early 1930s included the 16hp Viper (two litres capacity), and an eight-cylinder version of the 21/60.

The following years saw the introduction of synchromesh and a new 9hp model (1934), and pre-selector gearboxes (1935).

From 1933 all Wolseleys featured an illuminated badge in the centre of the upper part of the radiator grille. This unique identification light was to be fitted to all subsequent Wolseleys.

The Wolseley Wasp replaced the Nine, the Hornet engine was enlarged from 1.3 to 1.4 litres, and a 1600cc 14hp model was introduced in 1935, the engine powering the 80mph (128km/h) Hornet Special.

By mid-1936 (following rationalization after Wolseley was sold to Morris Motors in 1935) all Wolseley engines were overhead-valve units, fitted to up-market versions of equivalent Morris models.

The pre-World War II Wolseley Ten was powered by Morris's 10hp, 1.1-litre M-Series engine, but retained a separate chassis. A 1½-litre, 12hp four-cylinder model was also available, as well as a wide range of six-cylinder models between 14 and 25hp. The 18hp Wolseley was used as fast police transport.

Early post-war Wolseleys included the well-equipped overhead-valve Eight, with similar bodywork to the Morris Eight Series E, and the Ten. A luxurious 2½-litre Twenty-Five was built for a year from 1947. However, two new overhead-camshaft-engined designs, also based on Morris models, emerged for 1949; the smaller of the two being the four-cylinder 4/60, the larger, the six-cylinder 2.2-litre 6/80.

Top: 1939 Wolseley 10 saloon, 1140cc
Above: 1946 Wolseley 8 saloon

Below: The Wolseley Hornet of 1930 was a modestly priced small car, with a 1.3-litre, six-cylinder overhead camshaft engine. Few makers of the time could match the flexibility and power in so small a car.

The 4/44 was introduced in 1953, powered by the M.G. Y-type's 1250cc overhead-valve engine. The new model had coil-spring-and-wishbone front suspension and integral-construction bodywork, to be shared with M.G.'s ZA Magnette from 1954.

By 1952 Austin and Morris had merged to form B.M.C., and the group's 1489cc B-Series engine was employed from 1956, in the Wolseley 15/50. B.M.C.'s C-Series six-cylinder engine, of 2.6 litres capacity, was fitted to the new 6/90 in 1955. This model shared its body styling with the Riley Pathfinder of the same era.

The Wolseley 1500 was introduced in 1957, using the 1489cc B-Series engine, and the Morris Minor floorpan and front-suspension/steering design.

The Farina-styled 15/60 saloon was announced for 1959 and, in line with the rest of B.M.C.'s family of Farinas, was updated and fitted with a 1622cc version of the B-Series engine in 1962.

Top: 1952 Wolseley 6/80
Centre left: 1953 Wolseley 4/44
Centre right: 1956 6/90 Police Car
Right: 998cc Hornet, 1962

The larger, extremely well-equipped Farina-styled Wolseleys were the 6/99 of 1959, and the 6/110 of 1962.

The Wolseley Hornet, introduced for 1962, was a luxurious variant of the Mini, and featured an extended luggage boot. B.M.C.'s 1100 model was also given an opulent character in the Wolseley version, which was built from 1965, and replaced in 1967 by the 1300.

In the same year the front-wheel-drive, overhead-valve 18/85 was introduced, based on the large and comfortable Austin 1800.

In 1972 an overhead-camshaft, 2.2-litre, six-cylinder version of the same car – the Wolseley Six – was launched.

In early 1975, the wedge-shaped Wolseley 2200 was introduced, also with the overhead-camshaft six-cylinder engine. This was to be the very last Wolseley model, since it was renamed Princess by British Leyland from October 1975.

Above: Badge engineered 1969 Wolseley 1300 Mk II saloon
Right: 1966 Wolseley 6/110 Mk II with a 2.9-litre engine
Far right: 2.2 litre Wolseley Six, 1974/5
Bottom: The Wolseley 2200, renamed Princess from October 1975, continued in production until 1982.

Index

Photographic acknowledgements
The publishers wish to thank Neill Bruce, Nick Baldwin, the Haynes Publishing Group and the motor manufacturers and agents for their help in the illustration of these books. *Photographs were supplied by:* Neill Bruce, the Neill Bruce/Peter Roberts Collection, Nick Baldwin, Brian Crichton, Andy Willsheer and James Mann and by Alfa Romeo (Great Britain) Limited; Asia Motors; Aston Martin Lagonda Limited; Automobili Lamborghini SpA; BMW (GB) Limited; BMW AG; Bristol Cars; Buick Motor Division; Cadillac Motor Car Division; Chevrolet Motor Division; Chrysler Corporation; Citroën UK Limited; The Colt Car Company Limited; De Tomaso Modena SpA; Fiat Auto (UK) Limited; the Ford Motor Company Limited; FSO; GMC; General Motors Overseas Distribution Corporation; the Honda Motor Co. Ltd; Jaguar Cars Limited; Jensen Car Company Limited; Lada; Lancia Lancar Limited; Land Rover; Lexus; Lincoln-Mercury Division, Ford; Lotus; Marcos Sales Limited; Mazda Cars (UK) Limited; Mercedes-Benz (United Kingdom) Limited; Morgan Motor Company Limited; Nissan (UK) Limited; Officine Alfieri Maserati SpA; Oldsmobile Division, GMC; Peugeot Talbot Motor Co. Ltd.; Pontiac Motor Division, GMC; Porsche Cars Great Britain Limited; Proton; Reliant Motors Plc; Renault UK Limited; Rolls-Royce Motor Cars Limited; Rover Cars; Saab Great Britain Limited; SEAT Concessionaires (UK) Limited; Skoda (Great Britain) Limited; SsangYong Motors; Suzuki; Toyota; TVR Engineering Ltd.; V.A.G. (United Kingdom) Limited; Vauxhall Motors Ltd.; Volvo Concessionaires Ltd.